✳ *Praise*
MY DEAD P⌐⌐⌐⌐
ARE INTERESTING

"Zanily macabre, refreshingly irreverent, unimpeachably funny, Lenore Zion is living proof of Oscar Wilde's assertion that there are no dull subjects, only dull writers, because damn it, *her* dead pets *are* interesting. If Lenore Zion is what the future of writing looks like, rejoice, because not only is she a top-shelf writer, she's also really pretty."
  —Greg Olear, author of *Fathermucker* and *Totally Killer*

"This collection of stories made me squirm and applaud. Zion's fearless writing mirrors what's disgusting and great about the human condition."
  —Tony DuShane, author of *Confessions of a Teenage Jesus Jerk*

My Dead Pets are Interesting is reminiscent of David Sedaris' work in its wit, compassion, and honesty, but Zion's breathy, stream-of-consciousness, confessional style is all her own. She reveals her most disgusting, abnormal, humane, and hilarious thoughts on topics ranging from face cancer to elder care. Like me, she lies a lot in supermarkets, she's obsessed with the Dancing Plague of 1518, and someday, she'll be dead.
  —Summer Block

"Lenore Zion takes readers on a journey down the rabbit hole of the human condition. It is beautiful. It is ugly. And it is brilliant."
  —Tom Hansen, author of *American Junkie*

"Here's the thing about Lenore Zion. She's a hard and fast slap in the face. The kind you beg for over and over ... and over again. *My Dead Pets Are Interesting* is a collection of the most disquieting, riotous, surprisingly poignant and shockingly honest stories you will ever do yourself the favor of reading."
  —Kimberly M. Wetherell, award-winning filmmaker

"*My Dead Pets Are Interesting* is a really really funny book. I suspect a small camera has been installed in each copy, and every time we laugh, Zion is taking notes, plotting her next triumph ..."
  —Nathan Pensky

My Dead Pets Are Interesting

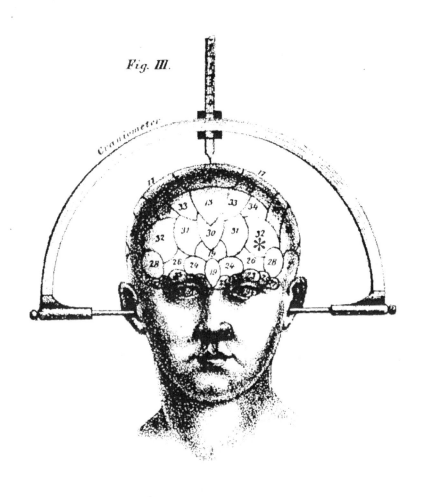

*

MY DEAD PETS
ARE INTERESTING

LENORE ZION

Published by The Nervous Breakdown Books
Los Angeles, California
www.thenervousbreakdown.com

First Edition, August 9, 2011
Copyright © 2011 Lenore Zion

Book Design: Charlotte Howard, CKH Design

Design, programming, and distribution for all digital editions:
Joseph Matheny of Hukilau.us

Cover Illustration from "An Examination of Phrenology; in two lec-
tures, delivered to the students of the Columbian College, District of
Columbia, February, 1837" by Thomas Sewall, M.D.

The text face is set in Cochin.

ISBN 978-0-9828598-3-4

Printed in the United States of America

For MEZ, wherever she be.

contents

foreword: lenore zion is not a whore 11

part i: i hate myself

that lady has a foot fungus 17

what not to do about rat mites 23

in the name of watermelon 27

sunday morning/the party's over 33

a relaxing day at the spa 39

stuff i've picked 45

a more unpleasant life 49

cognitive dissonance 57

on being a creepy adult 61

this is why i'm not listening 69

community service 77

part ii: just a bunch of kid stuff

what i did in my room 89

there have been many lies 95

squiggle wiggle all the way home 101

tallywacker karma with weiner vageener 105

no fur for the fifth grade mafia 113

death and me: a love story 119

the passion of the limbo lord   125

nana vs. the vagrants   131

spreading christmas cheer
is what little jewish girls are here for   139

we don't need no education   145

part iii: i'm not entirely certain

looking, living, fucking, fighting   155

the little-person incident   161

mass hysteria is still a big old question mark   165

boomie brown, sweetheart   169

part iv: dead animals

my dead pets are interesting   175

beauty in the eyes of a fish   179

early bedbug trauma   185

the jelly fish of christ   191

thanksgiving pig   197

a thousand words: baby birds   201

apocalyptic evacuations:
d.r. haney interviews lenore zion   207

acknowledgments   221

foreword:
lenore zion
is not a whore

LENORE ZION IS not a whore. Sometimes she says she is, but that's only when she's trying to impress you.

Lenore Zion is a sex-, food-, and blood-obsessed chronicler of the bizarre, disturbing, hilarious, and gross episodes of her life. Though she freely admits to having been a compulsive liar in the past, she's mercilessly honest in her telling of these stories, sparing no one, screwing everyone a little and herself a lot. Skewering, not screwing. Lenore is not a whore.

She freely admits that as a child she was a miniature entomological Mengele, torturing and killing insects under the guise of "scientific research." As an adolescent Christmas caroller, she fantasized about euthanizing the elderly. More recently, she bought a scooter and immediately drove it into a parked car.

Lenore Zion finds self-censorship difficult. Her id sits firmly in the driver's seat. She does and says stuff, and then ten minutes later, still pulling on its coat, her ego shows up to say, "What'd I miss?"

In *My Dead Pets Are Interesting*, Lenore tries to make small talk with her neighbor but can't help trying to convey the fact that she's not conceited about being in grad school: "I mean, I'm not stupid, but I make a lot of really bad decisions. Especially with men. Oh, my God, I make so many bad choices! Like this one guy, my friends and I called him 'The Face.' There's a reason. You don't need to know why. Or maybe … well, the reason is because he had this face that he made…."

One of my favorite sentences written in the English language is this, from "What Not to Do About Rat Mites":

> I was sitting there, basically naked, under profoundly unflattering light, complaining of rat mites, receiving a recommendation to remove my questionable, yucky, possibly diseased mole before its roots really took hold and it formed a personality of its own, and then I just started smiling at my doctor like an idiot, because for some reason I thought that all of this might have left him feeling sexually attracted to me.

It helps, too, that Lenore gets around. I don't mean she's a whore—she's not. I mean she gets out into the world; she gets involved. She mixes with her suicidal, one-legged Nana; her father the retinal surgeon and collector of sordid and violent art; her childhood pal Weiner Vageener; the Limbo Lord; her old, naked neighbors; and of course the "retarded dwarf" who chased her. ("Mentally disabled!" I tell her, uselessly.)

Finally, Lenore's writing does what all good writing should do: It consoles. Whatever stupid things I've said and done, whatever weird unpleasantness I might have encountered, it's not as stupid or weird as some story Lenore can dust off. Whatever antisocial thoughts I've had that I'd be ashamed to admit to anyone, Lenore has had them and freely admitted them. She feels the shame too, keenly, but then she shrugs and laughs, and suddenly wonders, "Is there cat shit on my hand?"

Jeremy Resnick
July 19, 2010

i hate myself

that lady has
a foot fungus

THERE'S A DISGUSTING commercial on the television. They keep flashing photographs of some unfortunate woman's foot—she appears to have a lot of trouble keeping the skin on her heels healthy. They're yellow and cracked, and frankly, they look diseased. But then, the product the commercial is pushing came into her life and now she has happy feet and she could maybe even be a foot model, and everyone knows that men want to date models, so she's pretty set. She doesn't have to worry about anything anymore, unless, of course, she doesn't want to be a foot model. Not every girl would want to spend the working hours having her feet photographed, day in and day out. Maybe she wanted to become an accountant. She might just really like numbers—you never know, not all girls are bad at math. If she were educated at a Montessori school in her formative years, the educators would have encouraged her to develop her natural skill set—they would have nurtured her true, instinctual interests by removing any roadblocks standing between her and her professional destiny. I guess this would mean the teacher would give the kid a calculator or an abacus or something and tell her to go nuts. If the woman really did always want to be a foot model, I suppose the obstacle standing in the way between her and her dream job would be this nauseating foot disease, so the teacher would probably have given her the product in the commercial and maybe shown her how to apply it. "Do it in little circles. No, smaller. Smaller. *Smaller.*" I don't really know what I'm talking about; I'm not a teacher.

I went to a Montessori school. The different wooden farm animals outside the door distinguished the classrooms from one another. There was a sheep and a cow and a duck—I'm pretty sure I have a memory of wanting to be in the duck room, and looking forward to the day that would happen. I don't remember doing any work while I was in the Montessori school. Unless I've imagined it, I don't think I did anything there but peel carrots and oranges. All day long, that's what I did in school. It makes me wonder what the hell my natural skill set is, if this is what I did while the teachers removed the obstacles that might stand in the way of my professional development. I suppose I was preparing diligently to obtain employment at Jamba Juice—and hey, that job might actually pay me more than what I'm doing now, if I worked my way up to becoming manager. And most people who go to Jamba Juice are in a really good mood because they're about to get some juice, and everyone likes juice. It's nice to work in a friendly environment.

My parents took me out of Montessori—or maybe I graduated from Montessori, I don't remember—and then I went to University Primary School, which was called Uni-Pri. It was the school associated with the University of Illinois, and I'm assuming it was also the school responsible for derailing me from my goals of becoming an orange and carrot peeler. Probably, because my interest in carrots and oranges was discouraged upon leaving Montessori, I repressed this urge to be active in food-related activities. This repression spawned an unconscious obsession with food, which would explain why I began sneaking extra fruit snacks (it's no coincidence I preferred the artificial orange flavor) when my parents weren't looking, and it would also explain why I'm unable to go more than five minutes without my brain screaming to me about food food food FOOD FOOD FOOD! I mean, what the hell do you people who don't think about food think about? Please tell me, maybe I can train myself to be like you. I'm so tired of thinking about food, and really, I'm tired of thinking about most of the crap I think about. Why does my hand feel dirty? I was petting the cat. Is the cat dirty? Cats clean themselves, so you're not supposed to wash them. But they clean themselves with their fucking tongues, and they stick their tongues in their assholes. Is there cat shit on my hand? Should I go buy some food? No one is looking. It's okay. I can have more food. You can confess to Facebook tomorrow if you feel guilty. Am I special? Do people think I'm special?

Meanwhile, as I was damaging my psyche with this repression, I was being changed. Uni-Pri, the school I actually remember quite fondly, was offering me up as a participant in psychological studies measuring child development and the like. I didn't know about this until I took a class in cognitive development, and we watched a video about object permanence. Object permanence is a concept children achieve at some early age—I'd tell you which age but I can't remember because it's not that important to me. If I ever get pregnant, I'm sure I'll suddenly care, and then I'll think it's the most important information in the world and I won't believe that some people out there don't care! What it is, is when a kid realizes that just because he can't see an object that doesn't mean it ceases to exist. So if you show him a toy, and he's all happy, then you hide the toy, a child who has achieved object permanence will cry and reach for the hidden toy and etcetera, while a child who has not achieved object permanence will be all "Whoa, that thing is just fucking gone now. It's just gone." It's easy to fool kids because their brains aren't fully developed yet. They can't be, otherwise they'd be so big that they'd destroy a woman's vagina on their way out. In any event, I was enrolled in a cognitive development class, and we watched a video about object permanence and, to my surprise, I was in that video. "Lenore, can you find the Snoopy doll?" they were asking me, and there I was, in a really cute little dress, representing, thank God, the kid who had achieved object permanence. How humiliating it would have been to be the slow kid in the educational video. "Did you ever involve me in any psychological studies?" I asked my father, and he said, "I don't know." It's okay with me, really. It's not like it's upsetting—all they were doing was having me locate a stupid doll.

But I do wonder if maybe this is why I ended up getting my doctorate in psychology. Because at the same time that I was being

deterred from developing and nurturing my natural skill set of peeling oranges and carrots, I was required to take part in psychological
studies. I was young, my brain wasn't fully developed—it couldn't
have been difficult to confuse me and replace "carrot peeling" with
"psychology." I really don't know what I'm talking about. What the
hell am I talking about? It's 2:10 AM between Friday and Saturday
and I'm just sitting around. I haven't even read a book or anything
tonight. I've just been sitting here, and my neighbor is serenading
me with his loud burping. I don't know why he isn't asleep. I can see
a number of lights on and televisions flickering in the neighborhood.
The middle of the night used to be so peaceful and quiet—it used
to be my time. This was *my* fucking time, and now everyone's wide
awake, burping out of their windows at me. I should really get a boyfriend or something. This is getting really fucking boring. I guess I
can read a book and stop all this complaining, do something proac-
tive about my lassitude—I mean, I'm a doctor of psychology, for crying out loud, but Jesus Christ, I just looked up and that diseased
foot commercial is on again. It must be cheap to buy air time in the
middle of the night between a Friday and a Saturday, and those foot
people are smart, because the only people who would see it are the
other slobs who didn't do anything at all other than sit around in
their pajamas from the night before, and those are the people who
probably get skin diseases on their feet. I hope I don't get one, but
hey, at least now I know what number to call if I do.

what not to do
about rat mites

MY DERMATOLOGIST WAS explaining to me that my problematic mole was likely going to have to go, but I wasn't listening much because I was focusing on the fact that I couldn't remember his name, and also because he was looking at me funny and I got the distinct impression that he was flirting with me, and I thought it was an odd time to choose to flirt with me, being that I was wearing only my underwear and he had just moments ago finished inspecting me for cancerous growths. I'm forced now to admit that it's possible he was only paying attention to me because my health insurance promises to pay him for doing exactly that, and perhaps my doctor was not actually attempting to bed me.

I hadn't even come in to the dermatologist's office because I was worried about skin cancer. The reason I was there was because I was ninety percent certain that I had rat mites in my apartment—my proof being a tiny bump on my finger that mysteriously disappeared in the hour before the appointment.

"I don't see anything," the dermatologist said to me as he looked at my finger under some sort of medical magnifying glass.

"It was there a minute ago," I said. "Look harder."

"There's nothing there," he said. "Take your clothes off."

So I had taken my clothes off and he was shining a light on my body, looking for signs of imminent death. I did my best not to look where he was looking, because those lights don't do you any favors and I've got a healthy enough dose of body dysmorphic disorder as it is without seeing every little detail under a special ugly lamp.

"We're gonna want to scoop that out," he said, pressing a mole-sizing ruler up against my face. "Ooh, yeah, that's gotta go."

Then he explained to me that, after the mole removal, the resulting scar might be more noticeable than the mole, because the human eye tends to disregard anything that is natural, and the scar that would be left over after he "scooped" my mole out of my face would be unnatural, and therefore more eye-catching.

"But I don't want an eye-catching scar on my face," I argued.

And that's when he smirked at me, which confused me and made me wonder if he was flirting with me. He kept the same smirk on his face as he described to me that the reason for the "scooping" was that moles are like trees and they have roots and if you just shave it off, it might grow back, like some sort of repulsive, tenacious facial tree made out of possible cancer.

"That's disgusting," I said.

"That's dermatology," he said. And then he laughed.

I thought that was kind of funny, not because of the joke, which I'm not entirely certain I can even identify as such, but because he was laughing while he told me about how if I didn't allow him to scoop the regenerating mole out of my face, it might eventually kill me.

If there's one thing I can always appreciate, it's an ill-timed laughing attack.

So I smiled at him and looked him in the eyes while he laughed. Then suddenly I'd done it for a beat too long, and I took note of his sudden break in eye contact, followed by his nervous and uncomfortable attempt to rapidly move on to the next dermatological concern.

I was sitting there, basically naked, under profoundly unflattering light, complaining of rat mites, receiving a recommendation to remove my questionable, yucky, possibly diseased mole before its roots really took hold and it formed a personality of its own, and then I just started smiling at my doctor like an idiot, because for some reason I thought that all of this might have left him feeling sexually attracted to me.

And this, I believe, is why he changed his mind and suggested that we "just watch" the mole instead of removing it. "Never mind, it's not so bad. I gotta go, but don't worry, I'll send the nurse in."

He was gone and out the door no more than ten seconds after he caught me smiling at him like a retarded person.

The nurse came in and told me I could leave. That's all she said. I wasn't told to make a follow-up appointment or anything.

Now I'm left wondering: *Do I have cancer? Is this mole going to kill me?* I don't know. For all I know, I'm dying right now. This mole is likely composed entirely of powerful death cells and it will take me at any time. Maybe tonight, maybe tomorrow, maybe in a month, a year, who knows? I don't.

So, I want you all to know that if this disgusting mole kills me, it's because I managed to put my doctor in a situation so socially uncomfortable that he was willing to take that risk, if for no other reason than to ensure a speedy exit from the room in which he was trapped with a creep.

I am a creep.

And it's killing me.

in the name
of watermelon

YOU PROBABLY GET hungry twice a day. Maybe three times. You get a sandwich or some pasta or a piece of meat or some fake meat if you're a vegetarian and you just feel too sorry for the widdle aminuls that would have to die to feed you. Then you eat the sandwich or pasta or meat or fake meat, and then you are satisfied. Maybe you smoke a cigarette, or don't smoke a cigarette because you aren't going to be manipulated by big tobacco because you're a smart, free-thinking individual, or maybe you were just never a smoker, in which case, you must not like to try new things.

The point is, you get hungry, and then you eat. Then you stop eating and that's that. You wait for the next meal.

I don't do that.

I sit around almost all day thinking about food. What do I want to eat? When do I want to eat it? How will I eat it? What will I not

eat? Why won't I eat it? I do this because I have an unhealthy relationship with food. Don't get me wrong—everything is okay. I'm
doing just fine. But food is my enemy, and I fucking hate it. It, in its
many forms, leaves me obsessed and bothered.

Right now, I am completely preoccupied with white cheddar popcorn. I have been thinking about white cheddar popcorn for about
five months. I frequently have to make trips to 7-Eleven in the middle of the night to fulfil my white cheddar popcorn requirements.
Purchasing multiple bags and stocking up is not helpful, because I
will eat every bag I buy on the day it is purchased. I don't care if I
am sick because I've eaten too much; if it's there, I'm eating it.

White cheddar popcorn is my enemy.

And I'm so ashamed. The guy at 7-Eleven thinks I'm a freak. I'm
there every day, buying this shit. Most people who go to 7-Eleven
daily are getting items that are actually addictive. Cigarettes.
Alcohol. I'm there getting white cheddar fucking popcorn.

This has happened before. When I was twenty-two, I had a watermelon problem. I couldn't stop myself from eating watermelon.
Every moment that passed, I thought about watermelon. I was at the
grocery store every day, buying myself watermelon, because 7-Eleven
doesn't carry them.

About a month passed, during which time I consumed between
twenty-one and thirty watermelons. And then one day, it came to my
attention that my habit had not gone unnoticed.

There was a girl who worked at the grocery store. She had her
bangs dyed purple and she wore a dog collar and she had a skull and
crossbones ring on her middle finger. If I were her mother, I would

have told her she looked fucking stupid, but I was just a grocery store customer, present only to buy a brand-new watermelon every day or so. My watermelon came rolling down the conveyor belt, and the girl looked up at me.

"Boy, you must really like watermelon," she said.

The little bitch. She said it like she was disgusted. Like I was doing something wrong. The subtext was: *Boy, you must really like watermelon, and that is a quality that makes me think less of you as a person.*

It wasn't as though I was buying multiple watermelons at once. At the time, I was buying exactly one watermelon unit. The only reason she would have commented on my apparent fondness for watermelon would be because she'd noticed the high frequency of watermelon purchase. She was keeping track.

The next day, I was back. Having eaten the watermelon that got me mocked by the little punk grocery bagger, I needed more. I didn't see her there, so I assumed I was safe. Out of range of her judgment. When I got to the produce section, I picked up a watermelon. Then I picked up another one. I figured that buying two at once would keep me away from the grocery store long enough for it to seem that my next watermelon purchase wasn't totally unreasonable.

I wheeled my cart up to the checkout lanes, and that's when I saw her. She was smiling at a male customer, probably explaining to him how and why his grocery selections were all embarrassing. The girl scratched her head with long, fake fingernails and shifted her weight from one leg to the other.

She wasn't there when I had come in. Apparently she'd been hiding when I entered the store, making herself discreet so that she could judge me and my watermelon. I went to the lane that had a longer wait, because she was bagging at the other one.

In a twist of grocery fate, the old lady in front of me asked the bagger in my lane for assistance in bringing her groceries to her car. My lane was baggerless, and the bitchy girl was bored, since her line was empty. The moment she looked over and noticed that there was work to be done, I started to panic. She walked slowly toward me and my two watermelons, a hint of malice sparkling in her eyes. She cracked her knuckles, one by one. I interpreted this as some kind of exaggerated hand preparation for the bagging she'd be doing for me, lifting those heavy watermelons and all.

"More watermelon? Hmm."

The "hmm" was what really annoyed me. What did it mean? Had she just gotten the proof she needed to justify some sort of consumer hypothesis? What did it *mean*? I panicked.

"Well, my kids really love it," I said.

Again, I was twenty-two. I didn't have kids. Still don't.

"You have kids?" she asked.

"Yes, three of them," I said. *Shit*, I thought. *Why did I say three? One, maybe, but three, definitely not.*

"Wow, three kids. You look so young," she said, trying to back me into a corner.

"I'm thirty-five," I said. *Thirty-five!* I was consistently told I looked younger than my age, and here I was, claiming to be thirteen years older than I really was to justify my watermelon to the little bagger punkette.

"You don't look thirty-five," she said.

I had to get the conversation away from my age before she demanded to see my driver's license.

"I figure that if my kids want something healthy like watermelon, I shouldn't discourage it," I said. It seemed like something a mother would say.

As I hurried out of the store, I thought that I had avoided disaster. I gave her a reasonable explanation for the large quantity of watermelon and it was possible that she bought it.

The next time I went in, I saw her there before I got to the checkout. Due to pure shame, I didn't pick up any watermelon.

"How are your kids?" the girl asked. "You should bring them with you."

I looked her in the eye, studied her expression. It was clear; I was being interrogated.

"Well two of them have discipline problems and one of them is in a wheelchair so it's easier to just leave him at home," I explained. *Jesus*.

"So the one in the wheelchair just stays at home all the time?" she asked.

"He doesn't like sunlight much anyway," I said.

I started sweating. Apparently, when pressured, I was the kind of mother who left her handicapped child alone in a dark room.

"Okay, then. Have a nice day," the girl said, absolutely with a touch of sarcasm.

I had managed to win the duel, but only by claiming something no person would claim unless it were true. My morals had sunk below those of a teenager with purple hair and a dog collar around her neck. She didn't even offer me help out. Not that I wanted it. She might have seen that my car had no trace of children. Then again, why would it, if I always left my children at home, locked in their rooms?

That night I ate both watermelons. I wished that I'd gotten a bag of cookies or some ice cream. But all I had were my watermelons, for which I'd created an entire abused family and aged thirteen years.

And now, I'm showing up at the 7-Eleven three blocks from my apartment at two in the morning, and buying white cheddar popcorn, plus a selection of other crap every time, so as to increase the odds that my white cheddar popcorn problem might be successfully buried beneath the pile of other assorted junk foods. But tonight, the guy at 7-Eleven made it clear that he was aware of my habit.

"Don't you cook?" he asked me.

"What?" I said, playing dumb.

"You only eat junk?" he asked.

"My friend is in the hospital, and she loves this stuff," I said.

He nodded at me. He smiled a knowing smile. *Yeah, sure, I bet your hospitalized friend is sending you for white cheddar popcorn at two in the morning, honey.* He didn't press for any more information, so I think I'm safe.

For now.

sunday morning/
the party's over

I CALL IT the Sunday Morning/The Party's Over Depression.

When I was a kid, my parents let me have birthday parties. An entire gaggle of prepubescent girls would swarm my house and play stupid games on Saturday. Most of these games don't have official names. There was the one where we pretended to put each other into some sort of supernatural spell, a possession of some kind, and even though we all faked it, we also all thought it was real when another girl was possessed. This always made me think there was something wrong with me. Why can't I become possessed? All the other girls can.

When some of the girls started to get sleepy, I'd take them downstairs to the kitchen and I'd open up the cabinet, take out the silver sugar container that was shaped like a tomato, and make everyone eat spoonfuls of sugar.

I was never tired. What was wrong with me? Why am I not tired? All the other girls are tired.

Then, eventually, everyone would sleep, regardless of the forced sugar intake. Even I would sleep.

And at seven in the morning, my mother and father began making pancakes with blueberries and bacon and eggs. I didn't want to be awake, but everyone else wanted to be awake. We'd eat breakfast, my mom would take pictures, and between eight and nine in the morning, parents would roll by the house and take their daughters away from me.

When the last girl left, I had to do homework.

Sunday Morning/The Party's Over.

Depression would set in.

At the kitchen table, my math book would be open. My notebook would be open. I'd spend as much time as humanly possible arranging my homework paraphernalia. Then I'd spend more time deciding on the format of my homework. Will I put a period after the number of the problem I'm doing? Or an end parentheses?

1.

1)

Maybe I will write the number and draw a circle around it?

Or encompass the number in a full parenthetical?

(1)

NOTHING LOOKS RIGHT. I HATE MATH. WHY DOES MY FATHER MAKE ME DO FIFTY MORE MATH PROBLEMS THAN THE TEACHER ASSIGNED?

When I got to middle school, the girls at my birthday party wanted to light matches. I wanted to light them, too, but then I wanted us to burn each other with the matches. They didn't want to do that. Didn't they want to know their limits? Why did I want to know my limits? What was wrong with me? They lit matches and put the tips into their mouths and breathed in, extinguishing the tiny flames. I tried and I burned my tongue. We all won that game.

Sunday morning came around, and this time I had a blister on my tongue to remind me of the party. I could feel it while I did my math homework. It reminded me that soon there would be another party.

I thought this Sunday Morning/The Party's Over Depression would leave me when I was over eighteen and I could do whatever I wanted. Instead, it extended its boundaries and began to apply to completed goals.

I graduated college. Sigh.

I learned how to row crew. Sigh.

I got a master's degree. Sigh.

I learned how to box. Sigh.

I got another master's degree. Sigh.

I trained for a marathon. Sigh.

I finished my dissertation. Sigh.

I got a doctorate.

BIG FUCKING SIGH.

This scares me.

Eventually, I hope to fall in love with a perfect man who falls in love with me, and then, if I don't fuck it up, stay in love. I know already that if I get lucky enough for this to happen to me, I can't have a wedding. I don't know if I can tolerate marriage, but I know for sure I can't tolerate a wedding.

Planning, excitement, choosing of whatever the hell you choose when you're planning a wedding. A dress, I suppose. Food. Flowers? Etcetera. Talking about the wedding. Thinking about the wedding. Everyone else forgets there's a life outside of the wedding, so people talk to you only about the wedding.

Then you have the wedding.

And then the party's over.

What a horrible way to start a life with someone. With that Sunday Morning/The Party's Over Depression.

So what I do is, I teach myself a million things. I learned everything about dogs. I don't know why. I like them, but I'm really more of a cat person. But I know everything about every dog breed. I know what medical conditions they are likely to develop, and at around what age. I know everything about palm trees. I know where they grow. I know what they look like, and which ones grow fastest and which ones grow slowly. I know about psychology. I know about people. I know about sexual deviance. I know about dissociation. I know about mania. I know there are an infinite number of topics that I can teach myself about, so I will never get bored, so it will be okay, it will be okay.

But now it's Sunday, and it smells like Sunday, and there's no one here, just me, and I kinda have a stomachache and I know that I have to go to sleep early tonight because I have to wake up early tomorrow. No spoonfuls of sugar for me, gotta sleep, gotta join the world, gotta produce and produce and produce.

So, I'm sitting here on Sunday morning, fighting that depression. I had a fun weekend. I went to a karaoke bar with a bunch of people I love and got a bit drunk and danced and then bruised the heel of my right foot, and now it hurts to walk, but I've got this bruise to remind me of the fun I had, and to remind me there will be another party soon.

a relaxing day
at the spa

I WENT TO a spa for the first time the other day.

Booked myself a massage and a facial at Burke Williams. It's very fancy, and when I checked in I was immediately escorted to the ladies' locker room, where there were Jacuzzi baths and showers and a sauna and a steam room and dozens of beauty products and expensive blow-dryers and fuzzy bathrobes and towels, all of which were available to me.

I'd been told when I made the reservations that I should come at noon, as this was when the spa opened, and I was free to spend the entire day there, soaking in various baths with other naked women.

My spa escort brought a number of rooms to my attention during the tour.

"This is the Silent Ladies' Room," she said. "You can come here and be quiet."

Inside, there was a woman being quiet.

"This is the lounge," she said. "You can sit here quietly."

Then she brought me to my locker and told me to get naked and please remember to wear my special spa slippers. "They're in your locker, along with your bathrobe."

I put on my bathrobe. It was very large, too large. I put on my spa slippers, which fit perfectly. I found this strange, because I am an average-sized female, but my feet are smaller than average.

I had an hour before my massage appointment, so I walked to the steam room. On the door was a large sign that said: DO NOT USE THE STEAM ROOM IF YOU ARE WEARING CONTACTS.

I was wearing contacts.

So I went to the sauna. Same sign on that door.

I noticed a bowl with bananas and apples. I hadn't been told anything about the bananas.

Could I have a banana?

I looked around me.

No one.

I quickly took a banana. I hid in one of the showers while I ate it, just in case.

It was still only 12:20 PM. My appointment wasn't until 1:00 PM. I walked around. Where were the other naked ladies?

I went to the Silent Ladies' Room.

I sat quietly for a moment.

I went to the lounge.

There were more bananas in the lounge.

I stared at the bananas for a moment, then grabbed one, unpeeled it, and ate it. Right there in the lounge. An employee walked by as I ate the banana. I got nervous and stuffed a giant piece into my mouth, just in case she was planning to take it away from me.

She didn't take the banana away from me, though, so I became bold and took another one and ate that right there in the lounge, too.

There was nothing to look at in the lounge. There was a fireplace, but I'd hardly call that entertainment.

Another lady in a bathrobe and special spa slippers entered the lounge. I got nervous in her presence, so I got up and went back to my locker to get my cell phone. Maybe I had some good e-mails.

No service.

I ate another locker room banana.

I went back to the lounge, and sat down. My masseuse walked in and asked if I was "Leonora."

"Yes," I said. Because there's really no point in correcting her.

She put her hand on my back and kept it there as she guided me to the massage room and spoke to me in a thick accent. This made me feel as though I were in trouble.

In the room, my masseuse told me to get naked.

Everyone wanted me to get naked.

She left, I got naked, she came back in.

"No, no, darling. You need to be on your stomach," she said.

I predicted she might want me on my stomach, but it seemed rude to have her enter the room with me not even facing her with a nice smile.

"Oh my goodness! So many tattoos on your body!" she said.

"Heh-heh, yes," I said.

"You have large bruises here," she said, poking my right butt cheek.

A few nights before, I let a stranger in striped pants and a feathered hat spank me with a riding crop, and he wasn't very gentle.

"Oh, ha, yes, that's because of this person, I don't know his name, and this event…. It's really not a big deal," I said.

Then massive amounts of oil were poured all over me.

As she rubbed me down, the masseuse verbally pointed out all of my bruises and scars.

"What happens here? You have bruise here, also," she said, holding my arm.

"I think I fell," I answered.

"You have scar here," she said, tapping my chin.

"Yes, yes, I drove a scooter into a parked car," I said.

"You have bruises, many bruises here," she said, holding my leg in the air.

"Right, I'm fairly certain I was sleepwalking," I said.

"Also many scars on toes," she said.

"Scooter accident again," I said.

This went on and on for the entire massage.

Then it was over. She told me to drink plenty of water and guided me back to the ladies' locker room with her hand on my back, telling me about how I should really use the steam room.

I had an hour before my facial.

I stood in the ladies' locker room. Now there were more naked ladies in there with me.

My contacts were still in, so I still didn't use the steam room.

I ate another banana.

I accidentally looked at a woman's bush for too long, and she caught me. I pretended I was looking at something behind her. *Hmm, that's interesting. What's that? A used towel? Interesting.*

I got into the Jacuzzi with two other naked women.

No one was speaking, even though we were not in the Silent Ladies' Room or the lounge, where we were free to sit quietly.

It made me uncomfortable, to not speak to my naked Jacuzzi partners, so I got out, put my robe back on, and ate another banana.

Then I went and sat in the lounge quietly. I pretended to be very relaxed.

The lady doing my facial came to retrieve me.

She also placed her hand on my back as we walked to the room.

We got to the room, and even though I was there for a facial, I was told to get naked again.

The lady smeared many delicious-smelling things on my face and then, for some reason, massaged my feet, which are not a part of my face at all.

As she was removing the face mask she'd applied to my skin, she tapped my chin.

"You have a scar here," she said.

Then I was brought back to the ladies' locker room with her hand on my back.

I took a long shower, and then dried off while trying not to stare at an old woman's naked body.

I put two bananas and an apple in my purse, and then left the locker room.

Many people put their hands on my back as I was walking out, all of them asking how my stay had been.

"Oh, very relaxing, just wonderful," I said. "Your bananas are very nice."

Parking was twenty-one dollars.

stuff i've picked

I LIED TO everybody except my best friend, Lisa, about how I'd gotten a massive scab on my chin. This was a couple of years ago now, but at the time, I told everyone I'd gotten drunk and fallen on my face, a lie that aroused suspicion in not a single person who heard it. What actually happened was that I'd aggressively made out with a particularly repulsive man whose face stubble had eaten through my skin until it was a bloody mess. Literally, a bloody mess. There was blood dripping down my chin at the end of this make-out session. It took more than a month and a half before my face healed.

Normally, I wouldn't lie about making out with a random guy, but this one wasn't someone I made out with for fun. He had a split tongue, like a snake, and there was really no way I wasn't going to make out with him. When a man has a split tongue, you must. You simply must. I don't know how else to describe it, other than that I didn't have a choice in the matter.

It was so fascinating that I allowed this making out to go on long enough that he scraped off my skin and I had to live with a disgusting wound that would crack open and gush blood once every three days. What can I say? I smile a lot, and when you smile, the giant scab on your chin is likely to split open. Plus, I'm a picker. I'll fuck with scabs until they're raw. I can't stop myself. When this make-out wound had gone a week without splitting, I went to see a movie with Lisa. I fucked with the scab through the whole movie, because the lights were out and nothing you do counts when the lights are out. At the end of the movie, I looked at my hand, covered in blood, and turned toward Lisa.

"Is it bad?" I asked.

"Dude, it isn't good," she said.

I actually think the movie was *There Will Be Blood*, come to think of it, and that's pretty funny.

There was also that time I sliced the tip of my finger off on a meat slicer in high school. I sliced the tip of my finger off, and I spent many months after picking off the scab that covered the tip-less area, letting it heal, then picking it again. Eventually it healed all the way, luckily for me, in the shape of a fingertip. I don't know how that worked out so well.

I just recently finished picking off all the scabs on my feet and toes from the scooter accident I was in. They weren't ready to be picked off, but I couldn't help it and I fucked with them until they had loose edges. Then I used a toenail clipper to clip off the edges of the scab, but I couldn't get a close enough cut, so I just ripped them off, painful as it was. Then they bled more, and now there are new, smaller scabs. I'll be getting at them soon, I imagine.

Another thing I do, another thing I can recognize as remarkably gross, is dig my fingernails into my gums until they bleed. I love this feeling. It's fantastic. It tingles and throbs, but never hurts. And then there's blood, bitter, metallic blood that seeps out over my teeth, and if I look in the mirror, it looks like I've been in a fight because my teeth have blood on them. Then I can make up a story for myself about how I got into a fight, what I did wrong to deserve to be punched until there was blood on my teeth. When I'm thinking about that, I don't have to be thinking about what's really happening, which is usually nothing, and I hate when nothing is happening. My fingernails are long, especially my pinkie nails, and people frequently tell me I have nice "coke nails," but I use them only for making my gums bleed. I don't do coke. I do drink Diet Coke, though.

Sometimes I think about things that make me cry, and I like this, too, because crying is romantic. But then I'll see my cats, Wetzel and Hege, and I'll think, *I can't let them see me cry. I have to be strong for them.* And this truly makes no sense at all. They don't give a flying fuck if I cry. And I don't have to be especially strong for them, anyway. They're cats. And I'm fake crying, so I'm not even showing legitimate weakness. Rather, I'm just living in a bizarre fantasyland and my cats, little assholes that they are, interrupted.

My friend's mother just came by my apartment building because my friend lives here, too, and I got really nervous. I always get nervous around my friends' parents. There wasn't even an exchange, but I got nervous anyway. I live in constant fear of offending people's parents. I once got nervous when I was at this friend's mother's house and made a point of telling her "I'm not a whore!" I wasn't being accused. I have no idea why I did that. I would try making my gums bleed at times like that, but it's kind of gross to watch. I know because I've watched myself in the mirror.

That guy with the split tongue was always nervous around me, the way I am around parents. The left half of his tongue would get curled under and he'd have to stick his tongue out and unfold it on his lips. He thought he was doing it subtly, but he wasn't. I suppose this is what a person lives with once he's split his tongue in the name of some sort of symbolic reptilian transformation.

He had just about everything on his body pierced—yes, including that part, and also parts you didn't know could be pierced. He had removed his nipple piercings because they bothered him and got infected. He said he picked at his infected nipples for months before they healed, and when they healed, he said he missed picking at them. I understand that. I'm already sad the scabs on my toes are going away. He was a really nice guy. I hope he's doing well, even though his stubble temporarily destroyed my face.

a more
unpleasant life

I LIKE TO pretend I was in a coma. Usually I imagine this coma lasted for almost an entire two weeks. That's a long time to be in a coma, but not so long that I'd have to let the possibility of brain damage enter my daydream. That's what my real-life doctors said when I asked them—they said any longer than two weeks is a bad, bad sign. And the nurses said it was too long a time, too. I'd asked them when I was in the hospital for (in real life) having driven my scooter into a parked car.

"Seth, my boy, I thought I'd lost you." That's what my Mom would have said to me all the time if I were a boy, which I also like to pretend. Or, actually, she would say it to me only half of the time because, in my imagination, my father moved away when I was ten years old, and then he never came back, so Mom had to be both my mother and my father. When fathers talk to their sons, they call them "my boy." So, half the time, when my mother was my father, she would tell me, "Seth, my boy, I thought I'd lost you." The other half of the time, when my mother was being my mother, she would just tell me, "Seth, I thought I'd lost you." I don't know why I like to pretend my father left us—I'm actually quite fond of my father. I also don't know why I like to pretend I'm male; males are disgusting.

In my imagination, this was all fifteen years ago. I would have been out of a coma for a long time, and Mom would still tell me that she thought she'd lost me. I guess my imaginary accident rattled her pretty bad, because the daydream doctors were saying I was going to die, that I had turned into a vegetable, and once a person turns into a vegetable, he can't turn back into a person. In my daydream, I take this "turning into a vegetable" metaphor literally, and I think I must not have made a full transformation, because I sure did wake up, and when I looked in the mirror, what I saw looked pretty human to me. What an idiot I am in my daydreams!

My imaginary sister, who is nothing like my real-life sister, called me dumb when I woke up from the coma because it took me almost a year before I was able to talk again. "I'm not dumb," I'd say. "You can't believe her." Kendra, my imaginary sister, she got married when she was only seventeen and then she got divorced and spent three years in the hospital. When I was in the coma, I spent a lot of time in the hospital, so I know what it's like in there. There are nice things about it. The nurses come in and smile at you, and sometimes they put their hair back and hold it all up with a pencil. They just put a pencil into their hair and somehow it stays put. I always liked it when they did that. For a boy (remember, I'm a boy in this daydream), nurses who put their hair back with a pencil are very attractive, and because I'm a boy, I am easily manipulated by women

I find attractive. That's the good part about being in the hospital—the attractive nurses with pencils in their hair, not the manipulation that is sexual attraction. But most of the time it's boring, and they don't let you leave. I don't know how she could believe it, but Kendra would always say that heaven was just a big hospital in the sky, floating on a cloud. If anyone's dumb, it's Kendra, for thinking that heaven is a building filled with people who won't let you leave. I don't care if that building is on a cloud. Anyway, Kendra isn't usually taken seriously, because of her stay in the mental hospital, which in my imagination is made out of golden bricks for absolutely no reason whatsoever. I suppose as a child I was really taken with pyrite, otherwise known as fool's gold, and I find it pleasant to think about a glimmering building with crazy people inside.

I was living with Mom. Actually, she lived with me. It was my house, because this is my daydream and it can be my house if I want it to be. I bought it myself, with the money I earned from *working*. I let Mom live with me because she was a good mother and it was the right thing to do. I couldn't let her live all alone once she got sick, which she is in my imagination. She, unfortunately, has some very aggressive but simultaneously slow-moving terminal illness, and her funeral will be a very emotional moment for me when that day comes. After all, I am her only son.

Even after she got sick, though, Mom was still up to her old tricks. She made me go out on a date with the daughter of some lady she knew from her weekly book club. My daydream mother freaking loves her book club. They're always reading those books for middle-aged women, the ones that become national best sellers because of how lonely middle-aged women are. They sit around in a

living room and cluck, cluck, cluck about the book, and then about
the neighbor's kid who—did you hear?—got arrested for shoplift-
ing! Anyway, one of my daydream mother's book club friends has a
daughter, and the daughter was a nurse, and because I talked about
the pretty nurses who smiled at me in the hospital when we spoke
about my coma, Mom thought I'd like her. And Mom was right; the
lady was pretty, even though she wasn't wearing her nurse uniform.
The nurse uniform would have helped, but she said wearing it outside of work made her feel self-conscious because men with fetishes
for nurses (the perverts!) gave her too much attention. In my daydream, I liked her. The lady didn't like me, though. It's because I'm
not interested in the same things as other people; I have particular
taste. It's not that most people hate what I like; it's that I like the
things most people are afraid of, which has the effect of making me
seem very mysterious and brave, but undatable. The sound of an
ambulance siren, the fire that's difficult to contain, the building being demolished—these things. I like to think about where the ambulance is going. Who are they rushing toward? What happened to
the person? Was he shot? Was he stabbed? Did he have a heart attack? Is he already dead? And I like to think about what the fire is
eating alive, what it's destroying. What is burning? A building? A
forest? An entire neighborhood? When buildings are being demolished, I like to imagine the precise point of impact that eventually
causes the foundation to shift so significantly that the building can
no longer stand upright. All of these things are of great interest to
me when I am a man who was in a coma in my daydreams. I'm sad
to say, in real life, I get sad when I hear an ambulance. I grind my
teeth when there's a big fire, and loud noises frighten me. But this

isn't real life—this is my daydream, and I can think whatever I want to think about sirens and fires and explosions.

And this is where I get frustrated, because I realize that the imaginary life I've created for my daydream is actually really terrible. It's depressing. My father left us, my mother's dying, I'm kind of stupid, my sister's a crazy bitch, and I get off on bad things happening. And worst of all, I'm a man. There is nothing I want less than a penis affixed to the area between my legs. What a bother it must be.

So, I switch. I'm back to being a woman. And now I'm in a restaurant with five men. Those five men are not always the same five men every time—they are chosen based on the men I currently find attractive and crush-worthy. These men sit around me, and we are having a lovely time. I am not dating any of them—we're just friends, and if dating is going to happen, it's in the future. We've all gotten together for drinks, though it certainly is an odd combination, as these five men are mostly unaware of each other in real life, and my general goal is to keep it that way, just in case I ever do really date any of them and decide to cheat on the one I'm dating with another one of these men. But this is a daydream, and I don't have to worry about those things in my daydream.

I'm sitting there, having a really nice time with these five men, and suddenly, there's another man, one I've been imagination-dating, but I'm not really very invested in the relationship. And let me tell you, this guy is pissed. He does not like seeing me there with these other men, even though in real life, I'm pretty sure this would appear to be perfectly innocent and go unpunished, as women who are cheating don't usually do so with five men at once—I don't even do that in my daydream. But in the fantasy, this man is very upset

to find me at the restaurant with five men, and he responds by becoming extremely possessive and jealous. I self-righteously tell him
that he doesn't own me! He doesn't even *know* me! He can just leave,
for all I care. But he does not want to leave. No indeed, he wants to
stay—and this is when he becomes violent. I can't explain why exactly he chooses to stab me with the fork he picks up from the table,
or why my mind chooses to have the daydream head in this direction. But this is exactly what he does—he stabs me with a fork, and
the whole scene gets very bloody.

Right about now, at this point in the daydream, things get tricky.
I don't want to emasculate the five daydream men I have real-life
crushes on, so I have to come up with a reason as to why they might
not come to my rescue at this moment. Simple shock at the circumstances unfolding before their eyes won't do—these are the fantasy
versions of these men, and fantasy men simply don't think slowly. So,
I need this other guy to be very physically threatening and evasive,
so as to excuse the five crushes for their failure to rescue me. Luckily,
I'm able to, in a quick motion, grab the man at his windpipe, which,
of course, brings him to his knees. Then I say something along the
lines of "If you ever touch me again, I will kill you. I won't call the
cops. I won't have you arrested. I'll just kill you, and before I do, I'll
castrate you. Do you understand? Nod your head so I know you understand." Meanwhile, blood is just streaming from my fork wound,
just streaming, but I am so strong that I don't even notice the pain.
I'm like Wonder Woman. Nothing can take me down. I know how
to bring a man to his knees by gripping his windpipe.

And then, once again, I realize that my daydream has turned
into what in real life would be some kind of a horrible, traumatic

experience. And I wonder why the hell I wasn't a man for this daydream, when having the physical strength of a man would really have come in handy? Why was I a man when I was daydreaming about being in a coma, when my masculine power was completely useless? Why are my daydreams so inconvenient?

In real life, I have never even had five crushes at the same time. In real life, I'm lucky to have one, and usually that one is totally unrealistic and impossible. He's someone I've never even met, unless buying a ticket to his concert and watching him perform counts. In real life, I've never been in a coma, and I'm fairly certain that any accident that might put me in a coma would be the death of me—I'm not much of a fighter. Every time I've been physically assaulted in real life, I've reacted by completely folding, waving a white flag immediately, instant surrender. In real life, when I finally fall asleep, I have dreams that I am trying to defend myself in a physical fight but I can't get the momentum up to make a punch really matter. My fists barely even come into contact with my assailant's jaw—they just gently tap him. I'm completely inadequate. I lose.

I'm beginning to think I like my real life better than my fantasy life, or the life I see in my dreams, despite the fact that I am infatuated with a dirty musician and not a normal man whom I met at a bar. At least my dad still loves me in my real life, and my sister is nice to me and never went crazy, and my mother doesn't have a terminal illness. And my name is Lenore, not Seth, and I love my name. And I don't have a yucky penis. Come to think of it, I have a lot to be thankful for. It might be time to start daydreaming about reality.

cognitive
dissonance

THE WOMAN SITTING next to me on the airplane was obese. Her side fat was hanging over the armrest, suctioning to my body like wet beef tenderloin. This was a six-hour flight, and I had intended to work on my dissertation, but this woman's stomach was invading my territory in a very distracting manner. It's hard to concentrate with a stranger's obesity problem sitting on your lap.

When I am touched by a man I don't know, or even just a man I don't know well, I instantly think of sex. Automatically, as this hypothetical man's hand brushes along my shoulder, I imagine what he might be like in bed, what parts of the female body he'd be partial to, if he'd do anything odd, if he'd suspiciously attend to my breasts as though he were an infant begging for milk. I can't help it. There's isn't a moment wherein I can decide not to consider the possible sexual result of a friendly gesture.

And, as it turns out, I can't help but imagine these same possibilities when a hefty, damp woman oozes over the armrest on an airplane to caress me with her gut.

Goddamnit, I thought.

Now I was fighting the urge to picture this beast naked and trying to breastfeed from my tits. I took out my dissertation materials in order to distract myself. Unfortunately, what I had with me was a book about sexual deviance because this is exactly the topic of my dissertation. Not a good distraction from what was now a raunchy and unwanted fantasy of being spanked by the fat lady, who was dressed as a Nazi soldier.

Nazis? I thought. *But I'm Jewish!*

I'd been conditioned to be especially susceptible to sexual thoughts on airplanes because on a previous flight I'd gotten into a discussion with an elderly woman who eventually confessed to me to engaging in sexual acts of an oral nature with her son-in-law. If that shattered-bone, old flamingo of a woman is swallowing her daughter's husband's cock on a regular basis, then this sticky fat woman next to me is party to some pretty bawdy aspects of sexuality for certain.

Formicophilia, I read. Sexual arousal to small creatures creeping on the body, especially around the genitals or anus. Small creatures like snails or ants.

That seemed likely for my tubby airplane friend. She already seemed slimy. Snail residue?

Now, of course, I was dealing with the images of her slimy, naked body crawling with snails, her bush not actually a bush, but a swarm of hectic ants.

Two of the things that frighten me most in this world are snails and ants. And now this woman was permitting these horrible creatures to sexually stimulate her. In my imagination, obviously, but my imagination is powerful.

I thought about that scene in *The Silence of the Lambs* where Clarice is walking down what looked like a dungeon, where they kept the criminally insane. There's a man who tells her he can "smell her cunt" before eventually flinging his ejaculate on her face in a climactic moment (for him).

That scene was genius in that it is the most horrific thing I can imagine happening to me, short of finding myself in exactly this predicament plus something else terrible directly after. It is the thought I reference when I feel uncomfortable in any situation. Therefore, general discomfort tends to leave me feeling oddly molested.

I was feeling molested. This woman could have told me she smelled my cunt while flinging a cup of semen at me and it wouldn't have seemed out of context. I was getting dizzy from the panic. At this point, I wanted nothing more than to have her suck her belly in and peel it from my skin so I could stop my brain from moving further in this direction.

And right then, she did just that. She leaned forward and tugged her stomach off my body and began searching through her carry-on bag, which was at her feet.

Oh God, what's she looking for? I thought. *What could this sick freak of a woman possibly be locating in her bag of tricks? What is she planning to do on this airplane?*

She pulled out a bag of strawberries. She looked at me with huge, nice eyes and held the bag up, offering to share them with me.

Then I realized: She's a nice woman. She's not the problem. I am. I'm the sick freak. And she wants to share her strawberries with me.

Epiphanies always seem to happen under stressful circumstances.

on being
a creepy adult

BEING AN ADULT, I've noticed, involves coveting the lives of those people who have not been around as long as we have. Their youth, the bounce in their step, their energy—Christ, their energy is incredible to me. They wake up early and they get showered and dressed and go on adventures, and before noon, they've lived more than I have in the past three years combined. They're at a lake, with a picnic of cookies and fruit and crackers and cheese, and they have an expensive camera and they all wear summer dresses they found at a thrift store in Brooklyn, and the boys they hang out with are all awkward— they don't come close to measuring up to these little creatures, these skinny little things. The boys have years to go before they catch up.

This is ridiculous, coming from me. I'm not even thirty. But I'm no teenager, either. I've developed an unfortunate, unshakable obsession with one teenage girl in particular. I've never met her, nor have I exchanged any words with her at any time. She added me as her friend on Facebook. There was no note accompanying her friend request. We have no friends in common. For the life of me, I can't figure out where she found me, or why she found me, but I accepted her friend request nonetheless, and now we are Internet friends. I frequently find myself trapped in a Facebook vortex, looking at her pictures, imagining what life would be like if I were this girl. She lives in New York City. I can tell her family is wealthy—even if she didn't list an exclusive private school as her institution of education, it would be obvious. All of her friends are wealthy, too—they go to school with her and they are multicultural and unique. Her pictures—there are hundreds of them—are uncommonly lighthearted and whimsical. This girl is a happy little thing, a very happy little thing, and I am profoundly jealous.

On *Law & Order*, the teenage daughters of wealthy New York businessmen and their trophy wives are always damaged goods. They do drugs—hard drugs, like heroin—and they are involved in bizarre sex crimes that result in the death of one of their tremendously good-looking friends. Their parents are vapid and neglectful, often away on vacation for weeks at a time, leaving the pauperized immigrant nannies to care for their emotionally fractured, sex- and drug-addicted daughters. Many times, after the girl is murdered, the derelict parents don't even fly home to pick up the corpse of their child until halfway through the show. It was just hard to get a flight home from the French Alps, or whatever.

I bet if my little Facebook friend were murdered, her parents would be at the police station within the hour. They'd bury her in a vintage dress with lace trim and a floral pattern, along with her five-billion-dollar camera that she loved so much. They're rich; they can afford to bury five billion dollars with a well-dressed cadaver.

My parents chose my name because they loved the Edgar Allan Poe poem "Lenore." The poem does not suit me—an unfortunate error in expectations on my parents' part, I suppose. One stanza:

Wretches! ye loved her for her wealth and hated her for her pride,
And when she fell in feeble health, ye blessed her—that she died!
How shall the ritual, then, be read? —the requiem how be sung
By you—by yours, the evil eye, —by yours, the slanderous tongue
That did to death the innocence that died, and died so young?

There are a number of reasons why this poem is inapt for me—for one thing, I have very little pride, which makes it difficult to believe anyone might hate me for it. But, in my mind, were my teenage friend to die young, it would be entirely appropriate to rename the poem so it was instead the name of this girl (which I will not mention out of authentic shame at my infatuation with her). Another stanza:

Peccavimus; but rave not thus! and let a Sabbath song
Go up to God so solemnly the dead may feel no wrong!
The sweet Lenore hath "gone before," with Hope, that flew beside,
Leaving thee wild for the dear child that should have been thy bride—
For her, the fair and debonnaire, that now so lowly lies,
The life upon her yellow hair but not within her eyes—
The life still there, upon her hair—the death upon her eyes.

My friend is not necessarily blond, but she's certainly closer to blond than I am. It upsets me that Poe's Lenore was a blonde—I have always wanted very badly to be fair and debonair, but alas, I am more accurately described as crass and primitive. This teenage girl, however, seems to possess sophistication by the boatload, which is confusing to me, given her age. Generally speaking, teenagers are awkward and unsure of themselves—they certainly have not, on average, developed any sense of self. At least, when I was a teenager, I hadn't yet done so. I vacillated between dressing like a hippie, sewing extra material into the ankles of my jeans so as to create bell-bottoms, and behaving like the child of a serial killer. "Look, everyone, I cut myself on a rusty nail that was sticking out of my desk! I'm bleeding everywhere! HAHAHA!" I suppose, part of my problem is the comparison I insist on drawing between this girl and myself at her age—humans, most of them, seem to share the tendency to look back upon themselves at this or that age with a tone of self-deprecation or humiliation. It's silly and irrational to be humiliated by events in the past, but we can't help it. We want to *change* things. We want a redo.

But why do we want another go at our past? How many of us, if given another chance, would actually correct our irrelevant mistakes? I'm not certain I would. The fact is, going back in time and doing it all over again wouldn't make a difference—I'd still be myself by the time I got back to the present tense. I can't change that, no matter how hard I try. What I want is to arrive at the present tense as the twenty-nine-year-old version of my lovely little Facebook friend, instead of the twenty-nine-year-old me, because certainly this girl, at my age, will be incredible. And I hope she knows that. And I hope she doesn't read this, and if she does read this, I hope that she knows that I am not a spooky stalker woman who sits in her apartment for days upon days without showering sometimes, staring at her Facebook pictures and talking to my creepy purebred cats as though they understand what I'm saying. Even though, to the untrained eye, this is exactly what I might appear to be. But I'm not. I'm really not. A wealthy New York teenager I am not, fair and debonair I am not, but I'm the best I can be.

What I find most disturbing about my infatuation with this girl is that, if her mother and father are divorced, it's not entirely unreasonable to assume that her father and I could begin dating. He's probably not out of my acceptable age range of dating—I'd imagine he's somewhere around forty-seven. If I dated him, this girl could be my stepdaughter. And I would want to hang out with her all the time, because I think she's so cool. I'd probably be dating her father mostly so that I could spend time with her. It's a very *Single White Female* sort of thing to consider. "What do you think of your stepmother?" her friends would ask, and she'd roll her eyes. "She's sorta clingy."

And I would be clingy. Her youth is so alluring, and I want it. A few days ago, I sat in my car outside of my place of employment and looked at myself in the mirror. I told myself over and over and over again that I was going to die. "One day, Lenore, you'll be dead. You will be dead, dead, dead and nothing will bring you back." I stared directly into my own eyes and told myself this, and I felt surprisingly comfortable with this statement of fact—I think I might have possibly hoped at one moment during my repetition that I would die *soon*, because then it would be done and I would no longer have to remind myself of the approach. But that was brief—mostly, I was consumed with the burst of love I had for this world and the people in it, including the young things that take photographs of their beautiful youth, and while I'm relatively comfortable with my eventual expiration and departure from this place I love so dearly, I wish desperately for an afterlife that might allow me to watch the world as it continues on without me. I wonder if it makes a difference whether I am buried in a box or burned to a pile of ashes or stuffed like a prized deer head hanging from a hunter's wall. I suppose I should study religion and see what the theological types have to say about that.

This is what this girl does to me, by the way. My intention was to write something funny about my covetous nature, something light-hearted and self-deprecating about my infatuation with her, but instead I've become melodramatic about my own upcoming death. You'd think I have a terminal disease, but unfortunately I appear to have no excuse for my theatrics. Simply put, I love this girl, and I love that the world created her. I hope someone loves that the world created me. I hope I'm not the only one who stares in the mirror and reminds herself of her mortality, and I hope I'm not the only one who thinks there's something beautiful about the temporary nature of life. Earth is such an interesting thing, constantly shedding its layers of life and replacing it with new ones. I want a pet dinosaur. That's hardly related, but I do feel it's appropriate at this point to mention it. Maybe I get one in the afterlife, when I am eternally a sweet girl in a vintage dress, having a picnic with my friends.

Of course, I know that if it were possible to own a dinosaur, that rich little girl would have one, and her pet dinosaur would almost certainly be a better dinosaur than my pet dinosaur. I would probably have gone to great lengths to ensure that my dinosaur was the best, and she would have effortlessly obtained the better dinosaur, and it would probably have a cute leash that she would unhook from its neck when they went to the lake together, and it would splash around adorably in the water, and my dinosaur would probably have diarrhea and then die. I'll probably go out in the same humiliating manner: covered in shit and flies and looking a bit sickly. And this girl will probably die like fucking Sleeping Beauty on a bed of wildflowers. Oh well, fuck it. As Popeye, who has nothing to do with any of this, says: "I yam what I yam."

this is why
i'm not listening

I'M HAVING A panic attack. Right now, as I write this. I don't know what's going on inside of me, because I'm not really panicking, as the term "panic attack" would suggest—instead I'm just moving really fast. Maybe that's also a bad way of describing it. I don't have a lot of energy. I couldn't go for a run right now if I wanted to. I have a bad cold—I've had it for days—and I can't really breathe through my nostrils. It's all mouth breathing for me at the moment. I feel like a stupid person, breathing through my mouth like this. I'm at my sister's house in New York. The toilets in her home have heated seats. This means that in the middle of the night when you get up to go pee, your butt cheeks aren't shocked by the cold seat—instead, they're soothed by the warm, inviting Japanese toilet seat that asks you if you'd care for a "front douche" when you're finished. No, thank you, warm toilet. I do not need a front douche. I'll handle this on my own.

So about two hours ago, right as this fast moving began, I was trying to take a nap but I realized that I couldn't really sleep or even focus my imagination efforts on one specific fantasy, which is how I usually operate. I get stuck on a particular fantasy for weeks at a time and I use it before I go to bed. This month, I've been thinking about all of the people who might be at my hospital bed when I get brutally attacked by a bodybuilder with a large handlebar mustache. There's my friend Jason—he's always there because he's such a good friend—and then I can't figure out the rest of the people because all of a sudden I'm focusing on this horrible image of being forced to breathe out of a straw, like a snorkel, but much smaller, and I can't pull enough oxygen through the straw to feel satisfied with each breath I take. So I start to have trouble breathing in real life, too, and my heart beats much faster and I wonder, in what appears to be perfectly serene inner dialogue: *Am I dying?* No, no, I am not dying. I'm just not focusing—there's a difference.

I have trouble focusing when I don't understand something. Earlier today, my brother-in-law, a doctor of particle physics, was trying to engage me in a conversation about the most efficient way to solve a maze with a group of people, wherein "solving" equals all group members pass through the maze, not just one member. Then there was a conversation about the Two Envelopes, which is apparently a big thing for mathematicians. If there is a number in each of the envelopes, and your goal is to get the envelope with the biggest number, but you don't know which number is in either envelope, apparently you can do better than a fifty-fifty chance of getting the higher number—it has something to do with making up an arbitrary number, and then guessing that that number is greater than one of the envelope numbers, and then drawing a graph and demonstrating the overlap that provides you with more than a probability of one, and then you win a million dollars in an envelope. That's my understanding of it at least. As he explained this envelope problem to me, I was struggling to even remember what the question was. "Are we still talking about the maze?" I asked, but no, we were talking about envelopes, or we could also be talking about two people locating each other at a mall with many stores in it, he explained. As it turns out, these envelopes with numbers and/or the two people trying to locate each other in a mall eventually made it so that my iPhone would work the way it does. I mostly use my iPhone for checking my e-mail and texting people. I don't know what envelopes have to do with it.

It was really hard for me to focus through that math problem, even though I wanted to learn it very badly. I really wanted to know it. My father would have understood the problem. I want to be just like my father. I want people to tell me I'm just like my father, to marvel at the fact that our similarities are so stunning. My father always wore wrinkled clothing to work—I remember with vivid detail each pair of suspenders he strapped over his shoulders before work every morning. I remember the khaki pants he wore, and the leather buttons that held the suspenders in place. His suspenders had mermaids on them, hot dogs on them. I thought suspenders with pictures of hot dogs were what dads wore to work. *Work must involve hot dogs*, I thought. My dad's work involved eyeballs, not hot dogs, and my dad didn't even eat hot dogs, but I suppose that some people eat hot dogs for lunch, even doctors. Doctors shouldn't eat hot dogs for lunch, in

my opinion—they shouldn't eat lunch at all. My dad didn't, and neither do I. My dad and I have coffee for lunch. Some days, when we
are unusually hungry, we have a banana.

When I'm at work, I wear skirts and dress pants and high heels
and I look professional, but I remember my father's hot dogs and
mermaids and there is nothing professional about hot dogs and mermaids. I usually tuck a tank top into my skirt and put a cardigan
over the tank top. One of my cardigans has a big hole in it, but you
can't tell because it is a black cardigan and my tank top is black, so it
disguises the hole. Though, even if someone noticed the hole, they'd
be smart not to say anything because the hole is directly over my
right breast, and if someone insisted that I wear clothing that isn't
destroyed, I could accuse them of causing me sexual discomfort for
having remarked on a garment flaw that happened to be directly over
my right breast. And that's big trouble.

One of the doctors in the hospital made a big deal about how
professional I looked last week and I quickly became humiliated—
I hate it when people remark on my appearance in that way. I hate
when people fawn over me as though I'm a china doll—*Oh my, so
professional, so fancy, so adult!* It's awful. It makes me want to hide in
my car where I know I don't look professional at all, because people judge other people based on the music they listen to, and I listen
to unprofessional music very loudly. Or the music is professional, in
that the people who made it are professional musicians, but it's not
classy music. Maybe it's not the music. Maybe it's the volume. But I
have bad hearing, so it's not my fault.

My father hates when people pay attention to him directly, too.
He doesn't like compliments, and he's unimpressed by any person

who finds him impressive. I, too, have been accused of "downplaying my accomplishments" but I don't believe I am downplaying them, and I also don't believe I am being modest. I truly believe that my accomplishments represent the bare minimum of what I am capable of, and anything less than what I've done with my life up to this point would be pitiful. Some days I feel like this—I don't know what exactly causes it, what the impetus is, but some days I feel as though I could do absolutely anything I wanted to do. I could become rich, I could become a leader, I could be anything and everything. And then some days I think I am repulsively insufficient, and I can't even go grocery shopping—I go to the grocery store and spend more than a hundred dollars and walk out with a bag of lotion, cat food, and soap. It's better that way, though, because I hate having food in my house. When there's food in the house, it's harder to avoid eating it all day, and I don't eat during the day, just like my father.

Some people have great big fat fathers, and those fathers sit around all day long, watching football and drinking beer and eating potato chips. I didn't have one of those, obviously, but I remember thinking that I was very lucky to have a nice thin father, one who didn't watch sports—when I went to my friend's house to play and her father was watching sports, I got depressed by the sound of football on his television. It reminded me of the end of something. Life, perhaps. The same depression would wash over me when I heard the musical cue for CNN News—it sounded like the sun had gone down and dinner was over and there was nothing left for me to do but math, fucking math, one math problem after another, over and over and over again, math. My father loved math, but I didn't. There was nothing I could do about it; I simply didn't love math. The

more math I did, the less I enjoyed it, the more I felt enslaved by the
numbers and the symbols, stuck, trapped at the kitchen table, with
the sound of CNN News in the background and my father leaning
over my shoulder, chewing loudly on beef jerky, asking me if I remembered the factoring trick he taught me. Did I remember? Did I
remember? Lenore, do you remember?

Of course I remembered. I did enough factoring to remember
for the rest of my life. But I forgot on purpose, because I thought
remembering something like that was sure to kill me. As much as I
wanted to be like my father, I couldn't accommodate his interests in
this particular case. I wanted to read novels. That was okay, but it
wasn't impressive. Anyone could read a book. Not everyone could
do complex mathematics. So if I wanted to be like my father, I'd do
math. But even he couldn't do some of the really advanced stuff—he
frequently shook his head and explained that he just wasn't smart
enough, but that I could be smart enough if I really worked at it. So,
in this case, I wanted not just to be *like* my father, but to be *better*
than my father. But I am not better than he is—my brother-in-law is
better than he is, in math, at least, and he understands things that
neither of us could ever understand.

I think this panic attack that involved no panic is winding down
now. Come to think of it, it might not have been a panic attack at all.
It might have been the double dose of cold medicine I took, hoping to
rid myself entirely of the unpleasant symptoms of a cold. Although
I'm visiting my sister and she's family, I still find myself feeling embarrassed by my need to blow my nose around her—as though blow-
ing my nose makes me unladylike and therefore a bad guest in her
home, possibly even a source of humiliation to her. Not only did I not

understand the math problem about the envelopes in the mall, but I've also been crudely depositing mucus into tissues all weekend. At this exact moment I am hiding from the adults, who are having an adult conversation, and I'm pretending to write, as though what I write is enough to provide an excuse for my lack of attendance to the adult conversation being had by a bunch of M.I.T.-educated people. It's okay, though. My father frequently retires to his bedroom when the conversation is just getting started—when he does it, he doesn't appear to be an embarrassment. Instead, he appears to be above it all, a person unexcited by the adult conversation. The master of rejecting you before you can reject him. I want to be just like him.

community service

YOU HAVE BEEN feeling insecure lately, concerning yourself with your community involvement. You catch yourself wondering whether you're contributing enough, doing your part, making the world a better place for people. Not that you particularly care about making the world better for people, but you know others would judge you harshly if you were to admit that you don't mind taking a passive role in the popular social battles, sitting back while others labor at promoting good environmental practices or whatnot, sometimes even allowing your laziness to reign supreme when you have garbage in your hand and no acceptable receptacle in which to deposit the garbage. "Litterbug!" a man yells at you, and no one you know personally is present, so you give him the finger, as your finger is completely free to express your reciprocal distaste for this man because you are no longer clinging to trash as he would have you do.

But, as mentioned, you're feeling insecure about this. So what you do is you decide it's time to *volunteer*. Volunteering is what good people spend their time doing, because good people are the only variety of people who don't mind coming in close physical contact with those yucky individuals who require free services. Bad people, like you are at heart, find it generally repulsive to ladle watered-down soup with floating chunks of potato into Styrofoam bowls for people boasting two months' worth of squalor on their skin. But you are trying to be a good person, so you sign up to do exactly that, because the first step to being a good person is behaving in the manner good people do. A man swats at flies, both real and imaginary, and you hand him his bowl of tasteless soup and, by unfortunate accident, his rotting finger brushes up against your finger, which is encased in a sterile rubber glove, but nevertheless you become convinced that the parasites that call this man home have been transferred to you, so you go to the filthy bathroom and vomit into the toilet in an attempt to rid yourself of the experience. It doesn't work, of course—at this point you are infested—and there's nothing you can do but go back to your good-person station and contract more rare illnesses from the hungry people who lost all their money in the stock market crash and reacted with crippling psychosis.

When you get home, you scrub fifteen layers of skin from your body in the shower and decide that there simply must be a less objectionable route to becoming a good person. Eventually, after hours of watching the flesh you scrubbed off in the shower heal, you experience an epiphany: Old people need help, too. Old people live in sad buildings with ambient television noise and they are simply *dying* for a young sprite to arrive in said building with a checkers board, ready to listen to a few hours of rambling, incoherent stories of the old days when stuff was just a dollar or a nickel or some small combination of coins. So you resign from your post at the soup kitchen and add your name to the list of people willing to perform the services that the older generation requires. This decision, you realize, affords you the incidental benefit of telling your peers that you have volunteered at both a soup kitchen *and* a nursing home—you are not a one-trick pony when it comes to social services. You are an auxiliary for *all* those in need. Because you are a good person.

And so, on your first day, you gather together your checkers board and a deck of cards and some dominos and you head to a nursing home with the name Sunny Isles or Sunshine Terrace or some such name with the word "sun," because nursing home titles must always include mention of the sun so as to avoid the other thing, the *night*, which reminds old people of their rapidly approaching deaths. The name Sunshine Villas allows nursing home residents to pretend they are at a resort in Mexico, like their granddaughters, who can be seen flashing their breasts to a twenty-nine-year-old cameraman in Cancun. One slight change—Sun*set* Villas—instead forces old people to envision a death, the fizzling out of an unimportant light, the sorts of deaths that make these old people wish they had exposed their breasts to cameramen in Mexico, because then they would have at least done *something*. But they did not, and one day soon they will just die, but not before you force them to play a few games of checkers with you.

At first you let the man win. He's old, how many thrills does he have left? So, even though he doesn't appear to know the rules of the game, you allow him to double-jump your checkers pieces in a way inconsistent with those jumping directives outlined in the checkers manual. But then, when he cheats his way to a win, instead of demonstrating the graciousness one might expect from an older gentleman, he gloats. "You little thing, you don't know *nothing*," he spits at you. On the next game, you take that motherfucker. You collect every last one of his checkers pieces and when you win, you collect all of your belongings and prepare to switch to another old person, one deserving of your attention. "You shouldn't gloat," you tell him as you pack up. "Now no one will play checkers with you." He shrugs as though he doesn't care, and somehow, though you are leaving him, you are the one who feels rejected. You shake it off. It is okay; you will find a new old person.

Your next old person doesn't have the manual dexterity to play checkers or a game of cards or dominos. He probably had a stroke, because he doesn't speak, either, which means no back talk. He smiles, and so you sit down with him. This isn't what you expected— his not being able to speak also means he cannot tell you about the old days when he had to carry his school books with a belt. But certainly this man is lonely, still, even though he cannot speak, so you begin to speak to him. You tell him your stories, like the time you got arrested for selling nitrous to another kid in middle school. "I was in so much trouble," you tell him, and he seems sleepy. Before you know it, you're treating the stroke victim as though he were your mute therapist—you're telling him everything, just everything. You tell him about who you irrationally hate, you tell him about the time you fucked your boyfriend's best friend, you tell him about how you're pretty sure you've been lying about the event you report as being your biggest childhood trauma, but, you tell him, if you are lying, you've been doing it for so long that you believe it yourself. You cry, because admitting this is emotional for you—you've never told anyone! At this point, something gets into you (you don't know what) but you just stand up and show him your breasts, like his granddaughter in Cancun, and you keep your shirt held up for over a minute, really allowing him to take a good look. And when you make yourself decent again, you can see he's happy. You've done some real community service.

The second time you visit the nursing home, you leave the checkers at home. Instead, you take a hat with you, and a bowtie, because you know that old men have fond memories of dressing formally, and you suspect your old person might like to wear a hat and a bowtie. Unfortunately, you cannot locate a bowtie designed to be taken seriously, so you settle on the oversized polka-dot bowtie you wore to a costume party years ago. Your impression is, the seriousness of the bowtie is irrelevant; your old person just wants to wear one. You arrive, and your old person is using the toilet, meaning, an orderly has lifted your old man's wrinkled body out of the wheelchair in which he was planted and then placed him on the toilet. Your old man has skin like a leopard, purple spots freckling his thighs and chest. The orderly stands, facing your old man, holding him in place because he might otherwise tip over. "Good job, Bill," the orderly says. "Come on, Bill, keep it up." Your old man swivels his head toward you and you briefly make eye contact. He closes his eyes and keeps them shut. You take this moment to contemplate suicide.

You wait outside for your old person to finish, because frankly it's rude to observe as another person uses the restroom, and also because witnessing the bathroom process in a nursing home has

caused you to want to blind yourself so you might never again witness something quite so bleak. Sitting on a bench outside is another
older gentleman, and he has no nose. There is a hole where normally
there would not be, right in the center of his face, giving him the
appearance of a two-month-old corpse. He's smoking a cigarette,
and you decide that his smoking has caused his nose to disappear—
perhaps it became cancerous and just fell off one morning. Or would
that be leprosy? You've never seen a man with no nose before, and
you try very hard not to stare. "Hello," you say to him, making a
point of looking in his eyes so he might think you are such a good
person and volunteer that you didn't even notice that he's missing
his nose. *Really? You haven't got a nose? Let me lean in and take a look….
Oh yes, I think I see what you're talking about. There's no nose right there. I
mean, don't worry about it. I wouldn't have noticed if you hadn't pointed it out.*
He nods at you in acknowledgment of your greeting. This is followed
by an extended period of awkward silence.

When you return, your old person has been placed back in his
wheelchair, and, oh boy, you realize that your old person looks depressed. This doesn't reflect well on your volunteer work at the
nursing home—the recipient of your attention must appear to be
benefiting in some way, otherwise there is significant reason to call
into question the quality of your volunteer work, and there is a list,
you know, a list of people who are desperate to switch volunteer po-
sitions from the soup kitchen to the nursing home. You must defend
your placement at the nursing home, lest you find yourself back at
the soup kitchen, toiling away at becoming a good person while being invaded by imaginary parasitic worms every couple of hours.
Immediately, you approach your old person and begin to dress him

up. You place the hat on his head, and you tie the oversized polka-dot bowtie around his neck. *Adorable*, you think. He smiles at you, and that's how you know you've done a good job. You relax, and begin to talk—this is what you've been looking forward to since the last visit ended. He's a good listener, due to the fact that he cannot speak or move on his own. You tell him about the man you last dated, and what a total jerk he was. Your old man agrees, naturally. You show him your breasts again, and then you take the hat off his head and the bowtie from his neck and tell him you'll see him again in a few days.

That night, you think about your old man, how adorable he was in the hat and bowtie, but you also think about the man with no nose. *He could use a volunteer*, you think. But you are devoted to an old person already and cannot jump from one old person to the next just because one happens to be missing his nose. You determine that you will bring the noseless man a gift, so he might feel attended to. On your way to the nursing home the next time, you stop and buy a rose, which you present to the leper who is reliably smoking a cigarette on his bench. "I've been thinking about you, and I hope you have a lovely day," you tell him. He hesitantly reaches up and accepts the rose, and you think he is much like a child, really—just shy and in need of affection, which you have delivered, thus cementing your place in the long line of good people who volunteered at this nursing home before you.

Inside, you dress up your old man in his favorite outfit again and tell him about your father, how he is such a strong man but you don't always know how to relate to him. This time, you show him your breasts for only a moment because time gets away from you while you are telling him about your father, and now you are in a hurry—you've got dinner plans.

You make sure to show your old man your breasts for an extra long time when you return two days later, and you bring him a nice tweed vest to wear in addition to his hat and bowtie, and also a corncob pipe to hold onto. You bring the noseless man another red rose, and hand it to him on his smoking bench. You continue to put your old man in outfits, even, at one point, locating a monocle for him (though it is difficult to keep it held against his eye, so you give up after a few attempts), and you continue to tell him all of your secrets and show him your breasts, and you continue to bring roses for the smoking leper outside—you do these things for months. You've really begun to settle into a good-person routine. You're feeling happier, less guilty about your tendency to litter, and you've not been infiltrated by a single parasite—or any other pestilent wormy thing—in the entire time you've been volunteering at the nursing home. This, you'd say, is a major success in community service.

And you think that, proudly, for a few more months, until one day, as you hand the noseless man his rose, you catch a look from one of the orderlies through the automatic glass door. It is, without a doubt, a look of bewilderment and disapproval. You realize at that moment just how cruel it might seem to give a fragrant flower to a man with no nose, week after week. In experiencing this realization, you also consider the possibility that you've been laboring under the misapprehension that your man is enjoying your visits, when, in reality, the manner in which you treat him is similar to the way a young girl plays with her favorite doll. You are dressing him up in costumes, for God's sake, and he cannot move to get away from you or speak to tell you to stop. Even worse, while you have been assuming your old man was delighted at the sight of your breasts, he may actually have felt molested by you. You never wanted to molest anyone; this was not your intention. You just wanted to be a good person. This is what you wanted, but the inherent badness inside of you would not allow it.

You stop volunteering at the nursing home and you return to the soup kitchen in order to punish yourself for your unintentional sins. And punish yourself you do, until you reach a breaking point and can no longer tolerate those individuals with horrendous green gums and irritatingly lacking conversational skills. You miss your old man—you don't want to tell the people at the soup kitchen anything. And so you work up the nerve to visit your old man, not in the volunteer capacity, but just as an old friend. When you finally do this, you arrive without a bowtie or a hat, without a single prop, because you want your old man to know he is not a joke to you, that you are no longer operating under the assumption that he might like being treated as a giant doll.

When you arrive at the nursing home ready to make up for your bad behavior, your old person is dead. You exit the building, entirely woebegone. The noseless man is outside smoking, and he doesn't make eye contact with you. You take a seat next to him. "I'm sorry I brought you flowers," you say to him, and he asks you in a labored long-term smoker's voice why you're sorry. You hesitate. "You have no nose," you say. He looks you directly in the eye and curls up his lip. "I can still smell, bitch," he says, and he walks inside, leaving you alone on the bench. You decide to never volunteer again.

just a bunch
of kid stuff

what i did
in my room

MY FIRST BOOM box was pale pink. It had a tape player and two speakers and an AM/FM radio. I never understood how to work the radio, but I did understand the tape player. This is what I used.

The boom box came in a package wrapped and tagged "To Lenore, From Nana." Mind you, my grandmother had nothing to do with this gift. My parents just put her name on the tag in order to both lighten the gift-shopping load on my mean-ass grandmother and to fool me into believing that the old bitch loved me at least a little. I wasn't fooled, though. She'd revealed her true nature the Christmas before, when my parents wrote her name on the tag for the Pound Puppies I so desperately wanted. Upon enthusiastically thanking her for buying me what I desired most in the world, she disowned any involvement in the gifting. "I don't even know what those things are," she said to me, looking at my new Pound Puppies with irrational hatred.

I knew she had nothing to do with my pink boom box. Like I cared, though. I had a new boom box, and that meant that my parents would be taking me on shopping trips to Coconuts Records to buy tapes. After all, what good is a boom box if you haven't got any music to play in it?

My mom and I walked up and down the aisles of Coconuts. She pulled out a Beatles tape and told me she thought it would be a good first choice.

"I don't like the Beatles," I said to her.

"No, honey. You like the Beatles. You don't like the Monkees," she said.

Actually, I didn't know of a single song by the Monkees, but I'd heard my parents discussing how awful they were when a neighbor bought his daughter one of their albums. "It's not the kind of music you want your kid to like," I remember my father saying.

Monkees = parental rejection. Understood. I did not like the Monkees.

But I damn well liked the Beatles. Liking the Beatles made me a good girl.

I also liked Joni Mitchell. I still like Joni Mitchell. That woman crawled into my heart and never left, let me tell you.

At the time, I must have listened to my Joni Mitchell tape, *Blue*, at least once a day. But I was young. I was very young. My attention span wasn't strong enough to last through the length of an entire album, so I routinely listened to the first six songs, skipping over the fifth song on the album, "Blue," because it was too slow and too sad, and the lyrics told me that "Everybody's saying that Hell's the hippest way to go." Even though immediately after Joni sang this, she made it clear that she disagreed ("Well, I don't think so"). I wasn't sure that I agreed with her, and this gave me an unpleasant feeling for which I was unprepared at that stage in life. So I fast-forwarded through that song and went straight from "Carey" to "California."

If I stood on my bed, I could see my entire body in the round mirror hanging over my desk. The mirror's frame was pink, like my boom box, and my big sister made fun of me for being so "girly." I loved it, though, and she and I were raised with different priorities. She was the firstborn, and therefore the weight of success was much heavier on her back than it was on mine. Successful people had no time to be girly, was the assumption. By the time I came around, I was expected to succeed, but it was okay for me to pause and be cute for a while instead of spending every moment of every day proving my aptitude for complex mathematics.

So I spent quite a lot of time being girly, and looking at my body in my pink mirror, singing along to Joni Mitchell's voice coming through my pink boom box. I did this so often that, I swear to you, when I listen to "California" now, the voice I sing along with is not my voice now—it's the voice of me when I was seven. It's unintentional, but I sound … cute.

Sometimes I wonder if it was strange for my parents to be sitting in another room, reading the paper or a book, hearing the sound of Joni Mitchell coming from my bedroom. Is it strange for parents when their young children begin to meet their own needs? I'd be there, alone in my room, and decide that I wanted to hear music. I didn't need their help anymore, not even in deciding what I'd listen to. Instead, I'd locate my Joni Mitchell tape, put it in, and press Play. They'd hear me singing along, dancing on my squeaky bed.

This seems extremely bizarre to me. That they'd be able to just stay put and not come watch as I entertained myself and self-soothed. Did they wonder what was going through my head as I sang in the mirror, staring at my body? If they ever snuck a peek, and I don't know that they did, they would have seen me awkwardly attempting to dance seductively.

To Joni fucking Mitchell.

If I were a parent, that would blow my mind. That must be one of the perks to having children. You get to see what another human does in his or her private time, before they are fully aware of societal rules that eventually force them to censor their behaviors when in the presence of others.

Though I hope my parents didn't come and watch me during those times. I hope that they just let me learn to be by myself, learn to do the things I would do by myself, without peeking in to observe. I love to think about myself at that age, before I knew what I should and shouldn't be humiliated by. That freedom disappears quickly, as I learned. Later, I began to sneak packages of fruit snacks to my room to eat in private, my own little secret snack, because I had learned that eating more than one needed was shameful. When my father moved my stationary bed during a rearranging, he and I discovered hundreds of wrappers from those fruit snacks stuffed beneath the frame of the bed. I had forgotten about them by this time, but as soon as I saw them I was quickly reminded of all the shame eating I did in private.

The thousands of times I listened to Joni Mitchell, I was unaware of any personality traits I might have been revealing about myself. I didn't know yet that letting people know who you are is a dangerous risk. I was just alone, doing what I wanted to do, and what I wanted to do was sing along to the same five songs that made me smile while dancing in my mirror.

there have been
many lies

I HAD A friend in grade school named Krista. I didn't like when she came over to play with me because when she was around I had to eat dry cat food.

It was my own fault. I told her I ate dry cat food, that I enjoyed it. It wasn't true. I don't know why I said it. She didn't believe me, so I had to prove it to her by, indeed, eating dry cat food in front of her.

It's not that the taste is so horrible. It's really a texture thing. It crumbles dryly in your mouth, and because the flavor isn't fantastic, your mouth doesn't respond with much saliva. The result is a mouthful of paste that tastes very little like the chicken dinner it claims to be.

A few years later, I was thrilled to discover that Krista and I would not be attending the same middle school, which meant our friendship would likely end and I would no longer feel compelled to eat dry cat food.

Within two months of middle school, however, I made the mistake of telling a select group of people that I was not human, but rather a very sophisticated robot. "Shut up!" they all said in disbelief. "It's true," I lied, smirking.

While living the robot lie, I was simultaneously working very hard to keep up a lie I'd told to another group of people: At night, when no one could see me, I would sprout wings and I could fly. They believed me because I was (and am still) able to do unnatural things with my shoulder bones. "The feathers come out of here," I said, gesturing to the tips of my freak bones. They nodded.

When I was very young, my parents told me that when I lied, my forehead would blink red and white. This is how they knew when I was lying, they told me.

"Why doesn't it blink when I lie to myself in the mirror?" I asked.

"Because you know you're lying," Dad said.

I believed it for only a few days. I lied to them on a number of occasions, and my forehead sure as shit didn't alert them of the facts. To be safe, however, I took the necessary precaution of sneaking into my mother's bathroom and chopping my hair crudely with a pair of old scissors, giving myself bangs to cover my treasonous forehead.

Later in life, when I was in college, I didn't really lie so much. On the other hand, I did have what I consider to be my most embarrassing moment resulting from my dishonesty at that time.

I was friends with a group of guys. The entire group was miserable, bitter, and mean. Frequently I became annoyed with them, because I was also miserable, bitter, and mean. One particular night, I drove to one of their houses, where we were all meeting for a lovely evening of being miserable, bitter, and mean to each other. At some point in the middle of the night, I decided that I felt like walking home. I told the guys I was leaving, but that I was walking. They urged me to drive.

"It's late, it's not a great neighborhood, it's dark, we'll worry about you."

I refused.

"Can we walk with you?" they asked.

"Fuck off," I said.

Miserable, bitter, mean.

I walked home. There were no incidents during the walk home. No one bothered me, I made it back in one piece, and I went to my bedroom. Then my phone started ringing. The guys were calling me to see that I'd arrived alive. *Ugh*, I thought, and I didn't answer. They continued to call me, over and over, and I continued to refuse the calls.

About twenty minutes later, I heard the three of them speaking to each other as they were walking up the stairs to my door. One of these guys was my roommate. He was going to open the door, and they would all flood in and annoy me. I wanted to be alone! Had I not made this clear enough to them? What assholes!

So, I hid. I hid under my desk.

They came in, and as I was hiding under my desk, I heard what they were saying.

"Do you think something happened? Where could she be?"

And then I realized that they were frightened for my safety. Yes, it seems obvious now that this is what they'd be all flustered about, but at the time, I was surprised. But, because I was miserable, bitter, and mean, I wasn't touched by their concern. I was annoyed.

Fuck those guys, I thought. *I'm going to stay right here under my desk and they can act like hysterical women for as long as they want.*

They called a few of my other friends, asking around. One of them walked in my room. I held my breath as his legs moved by my hiding place. It was at this moment that I realized that what I was doing was really stupid. Really, really stupid. But I was locked in now—no way out. Or no way out that included the preservation of my dignity.

This went on for quite some time. Eventually, I realized that they weren't leaving. They weren't calming down. If anything, their panic was escalating. I had one option, and that was to emerge from my pathetic hiding place and approach them with my tail between my legs.

So I did. And they were very angry. One of them even shoved me, but that was only because he was in love with me and he was reacting strongly to the realization that he was in love with a stupid cunt.

People do silly things for silly reasons. Even after they grow up, they continue to do silly things for silly reasons. And, at least in my case, when I've looked at some of the things I've done, I deal with enough self-hatred and embarrassment that I don't really need to be encouraged to reflect upon those actions critically. I already know I'm an idiot. I've known for quite some time.

I think the lies people tell are indicative of the world they'd prefer to live in to reality. If I could indeed sprout wings at night when no one was looking, I'd want for nothing. Similarly, having a complex system of wires and blinking lights beneath my skin seems a much more lovely existence than what is real, which is sticky, clogged organs and a mess of blood.

And while I certainly would like to maintain my diet of human food as opposed to dry cat food, I do wish that I favored the stuff for cats. It's cheaper.

Lies will get you into trouble. But a world without lies is a bland, bland world.

squiggle wiggle all the way home

WHEN I WAS a kid, my mother purchased for me a short-lived product called a Squiggle Wiggle Writer. The Squiggle Wiggle Writer was a pen with a little motor that spun around at the top, causing a vibration, or a wiggle. The result: Instead of a straight line, the pen produced a squiggle. I used to write my name millions of times when I was younger, like girls do with the names of boys they have crushes on, only I was at the time, and continue to be, a narcissist, so I wrote only my own name. *Lenore Lenore Lenore Lenore.*

It's important to point out that my cat just vomited on my foot. My goal is to ignore the barf until I finish writing what I set out to write, because … I'm not really sure why. It's good to have goals.

With the Squiggle Wiggle Writer, my name was textured and plump. The pen was satisfying to write with. It was good for penmanship. But more important for a narcissist, the Squiggle Wiggle Writer filled a much more important function; it allowed me to fuck myself.

The Squiggle Wiggle Writer was my very first vibrator. It was a sex toy for kids—a wildly brilliant idea, though the market apparently did not reflect the genius of the design, given its curt appearance in toy stores. I have to believe that the manufacturers of this product knew exactly what they were pumping out of their assembly lines, much in the same way the makers of those massage tools at Sharper Image know damn well what they're selling. People just don't need a handheld back massager, and even if the thing is purchased with the intention of massaging one's back, eventually it will find its way downtown.

My cat is now lapping up his own vomit from my foot. Cats tend to do this for some reason. You'd think the stomach acid would act as a deterrent, but not so for felines.

Similarly, people don't need pens that wiggle. We don't need to write in a squiggle. We do, however, need to get off. Unless we're really religious, and then we are filled with God orgasms. Spiritual, divine, Godgasms.

I was raised without religion, so I needed a vibrator.

My Squiggle Wiggle Writer was not the only one in the household as I grew up. My brother had been given one as well. I'm fairly certain that he similarly employed his personal Squiggle Wiggle Writer, something to the tune of holding it up against his balls while he beat off. While my parents are no idiots, I do sometimes wonder if they were aware of the masturbatory treasures they'd offered us.

I also sometimes wonder if, in order to protect my fragile psyche, I created the extra Squiggle Wiggle Writer that belonged to my brother. I wonder if perhaps there was but one in the entire house, and this one Squiggle Wiggle Writer was abused by both my brother and me. Did I share my very first vibrator with my brother? I'll never know.

This kitty puke is starting to get really gross. There are patches of it missing from my cat's taste testing, and now I'm concerned my cat's rough tongue served as a grinding agent, really working the barf elements into my skin.

The first nonmanual methods of masturbation. Sometimes you get lucky and get a vibrator disguised as a pen. Other times you don't, and you spend the first seven years of your sexual awakening fucking an electric toothbrush or a tube sock filled with your sister's hand lotion.

Screw it. I'm going to wash my foot.

tallywacker karma
with weiner vageener

AS A CHILD, I remember being bored by most of my playmate options. I had fun with my brothers, so there wasn't much need for outside interaction.

That changed when I met Gina. There was something different about Gina. I liked her immediately. She was quiet. She was timorous. She didn't have strong opinions. Mostly, though, what I liked about her was that she was malleable. Being friends with Gina was like having a life-sized doll to whom I could shrewdly transfer guilt in sticky situations.

"Who cut a big hole in the hammock?"

"Gina did."

"Who spilled chocolate milk on the carpet and then covered it up with my silk scarf?"

"Gina did."

"Who wrote 'Mom smells like poop' on the living room wall with brown permanent marker?"

"Gina did."

"Gina, did you write 'Mom smells like poop' on the living room wall?"

"Yes, Mrs. Zion," Gina would confess.

"Do you mean *your* mom smells like poop, or were you referring to me?"

Gina would look at me for help. I'd subtly nod over to my mom.

"I meant you, Mrs. Zion. You smell like poop," Gina would say, utterly subjugated.

Worked every time.

The first time I went to Gina's house, I was taken aback. It was nothing like mine. Her parents didn't talk much. There wasn't much art on the walls, and anything that was hanging was a landscape scene. My house was filled with bizarre paintings, many of the pieces sordid or violent in nature. Even perverted in nature. The landscape paintings on Gina's walls didn't have any aggressive connotations. They didn't even have hidden genitals! They were landscapes, and that was it.

Their kitchen was filled with strange foods I'd never heard of. There were Kraft Singles, packages of Hamburger Helper, Rice-A-Roni, Fruit Roll-Ups, and more. My kitchen had wedges of brie, French-cut rack of lamb, long-grain brown rice, and all-natural fruit bars.

In Gina's house, there was always the faint sound of football in the background, even when it wasn't football season. Even when, I swear, the television wasn't on. Like ghost football. Listening to the conversations held in Gina's home was like witnessing the interactions of an alien life form. The first time I ate dinner at their house, we had hot dogs.

We didn't eat hot dogs in my house.

"Bob called today," her dad said.

"What did he have to say?" her mother responded.

"Oh, this and that," he answered.

This and that? What does it mean? I wondered.

"How're Joan and Rick?" Gina's mother asked.

She wants to know more? Why would she want to know more? I thought.

"Oh, they're good," he said.

"Joan and Rick are Gina's cousins, Lenore. They're about your age," Gina's mother told me while handing me a can of nondiet, full-sugar Coke.

What kind of people name their children Joan and Rick? They sound like middle-aged schlubs. Did they come out of the womb as accountants, with their calculators and fountain pens ready to go? I nodded to Gina's mother and popped open my Coke. The elusive and sought-after red can…. I would have to brag about this indulgence to my brothers when I got home.

"Yup," Gina's dad said.

"Yup," Gina's mom said.

"Yup," Gina's little brother said.

"Yup," Gina said.

They all looked at me. I gulped my Coke:

"Yup?"

That satisfied them. There was no punching at the table, no name-calling, no cussing. There was no graphic talk of eye surgery, no filthy jokes about diarrhea and anal sex. It was Midwestern whole-some behavior in action, right before my very own eyes.

Gina didn't have any older siblings. I had three of them, so I'd learned all about the bad words and what a penis was and what a vagina was, and how those two things could be used together. When my siblings and I would joke about wieners and balls, Gina was in the dark. After dinner at her house, it occurred to me that, given her lack of knowledge in those areas, she might not serve as a plausible scapegoat in the most problematic of situations. I took it upon my-self to educate Gina.

"Fuck," I said.

"Fuck," Gina repeated.

"Ass."

"Ass."

"Cunt."

"Cunt?"

"Very good. It's a bad way of saying 'mouth,'" I told her, sensing her confusion.

"Can you use it in a sentence?" Gina asked.

"Your mother will be appalled by the words coming out of your cunt," I offered.

"Got it," Gina said, smiling with the pride of hard-earned comprehension.

Within a few weeks, Gina had a brand-new vocabulary, and it was all thanks to my leadership. She did find the word "vagina" a bit tricky at first, stumbling and calling it a "puhg-eye-nuh," but even-tually she got the hang of it. When she had mastered the entire list, my brothers and I held a graduation ceremony for her in which we awarded her with a black belt (literally) and sanctioned for her the new moniker "Weiner Vageener" for use in the absence of leering adults. It was a proud day for us all.

I had another neighbor; the elderly, sweet, brownie-baking, tulip-planting, cheek-squeezing Mrs. Scribner. She used to invite us into her home and feed us fresh-from-the-oven oatmeal raisin cookies, much in the same way a naively compassionate woman would invite a certifiably insane rapist into her home in the middle of the night because it was raining outside. We'd sit at her kitchen table, downing one cookie after another, acting like angels, just waiting for her to need to use the bathroom. That never took long, of course, because old people have tiny bladders. Something about aging shrivels that whole system down so a tri-hourly trip to the bathroom is necessary for basic comfort. As soon as we heard the bathroom door close, we'd go run through her house. We'd take her little glass figurines of deer, her silverware, her doilies, the quilts, and we'd rearrange them. Just put 'em somewhere else altogether. Just to confuse the poor old lady.

One day, Mrs. Scribner was outside with her little gardening gloves on. They had a daisy pattern, if I remember correctly, and they snapped at the wrist. She was digging in the garden, planting bulbs. She seemed to be completely at peace.

Tim, Gina, and I watched her from the swing set.

"We should mess with her," Tim said.

"You're right. We should," I agreed.

"What should we do?" Tim asked.

"I don't know. Let me think," I said.

"We could show her our paginas!" Gina suggested.

"For the last time, Gina, vagina, not pagina. But that's not a bad idea," I said.

"I don't have a vagina," Tim said.

"You could show her your tallywacker," Gina said.

"It's true, you could," I said swelling with pride at Gina's newly acquired vocabulary.

We got as close as we could to Mrs. Scribner, the three of us, standing in a row. She didn't realize we were there, just hovering nearby diabolically. Then we looked at one another and nodded.

"*Hey, Mrs. Scribner!*" we shouted, all at once.

Then we dropped our pants, and wiggled our little genitals at her. Tallywackers and paginas all over the place, sun shining on our privates like direct streams of light from God.

Mrs. Scribner dropped her gardening spade and covered her mouth. We laughed and laughed and laughed.

"That's right! Cover your cunt, Mrs. Scribner!" I yelled.

"Cover your cunt! Cover your cunt!" Gina repeated, over and over again. In fact, she was still repeating it when her mother drove by and saw the three of us with our pants down and our genitals directed at a horrified Mrs. Scribner.

Gina was in big trouble. And Tim and I told our parents, truthfully this time, that it was Gina's idea. Poor Weiner Vageener, she never saw it coming.

Though I did get her into big trouble a lot when we were in grade school, Gina still wanted to be friends with me in junior high. Shockingly, her parents allowed our continued contact. One summer day when we were eleven, she and I were walking to the pool in our bikinis, which were far from being filled out, as we were both late developers. A big, obese, forty-something man in a tiny little car drove by us slowly.

"That was weird," Gina said.

He sped forward, pulled into a driveway, and turned his car around so it was facing us. Then he drove back to us, even more slowly, while doing something that we couldn't quite make out. As he got closer and closer, he sharply reclined his seat and lifted his enormous gut up to the window, eventually revealing his flaccid penis, which was flopped over his left leg.

"*Uuugghhhnnnnggghhh!*" he moaned at us, making eye contact.

He waited for our reactions, and when he got what he was searching for, which must have been the look of pure anguish on our faces, he whipped his penis back between his legs and lowered his body back into his seat. Then he sped off.

Karma's a bitch.

no fur for the fifth grade mafia

IN THIRD GRADE, I came home from school crying. Some kids on the bus had teased me about my brown hair, calling me mousy. My bus was made up of kids from kindergarten through fifth grade, but the fat cats of the bus were a group of nasty fifth graders, drunk with the sweet power of being the oldest.

"It's not fair, Mom," I whined to her willing ears. "I hate my boring, ugly, brown hair."

"Well, Joanna from down the street is bald because she has cancer. Would you rather be bald and dying of cancer like Joanna from down the street?"

"Yes," I said.

And I meant it. If I were like Joanna from down the street, dying of cancer, people would feel sorry for me. That sounded wonderful.

"I think you'd be pretty sad if you got cancer, Lenore. I think you'd be wishing for your brown hair every day and every night, and crying yourself to sleep when you didn't get it," Mom said. "Then, while the chemotherapy was keeping you hunched over the toilet, vomiting your insides out, and your face was swollen from irritation, and you were covered in sores from radiation, well, then I think you'd wish you had your brown hair back."

Stupid Joanna, I thought.

I wished I could be just like those fifth graders. I had wanted to be friends with them. It was impossible now. No longer feasible. Not now that I knew how they felt about my hair.

That evening, I watched my mother as she primped and made herself beautiful for her date with my father. She sat at her vanity combing through her stick-straight, brown, shiny hair. Prettier than mine, definitely. She was telling me what she would order from the restaurant in an exaggerated, excited voice.

"Duck breast, sliced into pieces. The pieces will be laid one on top of the other, on top of the other, on top of the other. They are all going to have that thin piece of fat on the top, the piece Daddy likes to leave on and eat, but I'll cut it off. They are going to drizzle a cherry sauce over all of the pieces, and each bite will be so delicious," she said.

Then she held her comb in her fist and pulled her hands to her chest, right in front of her heart. She took a deep breath in.

"Lenore, it's going to be marvelous."

She zipped up her knee-high leather boots and grabbed for my hand. We walked to the front hall, where there was a walk-in closet. She pulled a floor-length fur coat off a hanger and pulled it around herself. It swallowed her up whole, and she looked so beautiful and glamorous. She looked superior. And she marched like a queen out into the kitchen, where my father was sipping a glass of red wine, waiting for her. Pre-drinking, he called it.

"Heard you had a bad day today, sweetheart," my dad said.

"I want a fur coat like Mom's," I said.

"Must have been some bad day," he said.

"There are some kids making fun of her. They think they're better than she is, I guess," my mother explained to Dad.

"They're incorrect," my father said.

Because he said "incorrect" instead of "wrong," it sounded very scientific. As though he'd done a study and concluded that the fifth graders were, in fact, not better than his child. I believed it.

I was very spoiled, so that Christmas, I not only unwrapped a rabbit fur coat but a matching rabbit fur muffler and rabbit fur earmuffs to wear with it.

"Put it on, Lenore," my mother said, smiling. "Model it for us!"

I slid my arms into my new fur coat and hugged myself, brushing my hands up and down the silky fur. It felt cold on the outside and warm on the inside, so that anybody who tried to touch me would freeze, but inside, I'd be warm and protected.

"These, too," my dad said, holding up the muffler and earmuffs.

When my hands were tucked inside the muffler and the black, shining fur coat was around my body, I looked like an illustration of a British children's book about a wealthy orphan. And my brown hair sure as shit didn't look boring and mousy when it was poking through rabbit fur earmuffs.

From the moment I had unwrapped the rabbit fur coat and the matching accessories I'd wanted to show them off to the nasty fifth graders who thought I was boring. I couldn't wait to see their faces when I walked up the steps of the bus, enveloped by beauty and superiority, and marched down the aisle of the bus in the same royal way my mother had marched into the kitchen before she went out to eat her perfectly trimmed, cherry-flavored duck breast. I begged my mother to pack me a bagged lunch of duck breast for that first day back to school, but she told me I'd have to settle for my usual ham sandwich.

Victory seemed inevitable; the fifth graders didn't have fur coats and I did. If I had been just a few years older, I could have also worn bright red lipstick, which would really have demonstrated my sophistication and ascendancy.

I woke up early, too excited to sleep. I was the first person at my bus stop, bundled in my eye-catching coat, with the earmuffs clinging to my ears and my tiny hands stuffed into the furry muffler. I saw the bus coming around the curves of my winding, residential street. The moment of truth was approaching.

I stepped onto the bus, and there they all were, trading pencils. That was the big thing back then. Pencils were much like currency. My mother had special-ordered pencils with my full name engraved on the sides for me. "Lenore Margot Zion" carved into each and every pencil in gold lettering. These, while exclusive, were difficult to trade, as Lenore Margot Zion is a rare name and there were very few of us in the area.

I stuck my head into the air, making sure not to look at the fifth graders. The first few seconds of walking down the aisle of the school bus were nothing short of bliss. *I'm winning*, I thought.

Then the fantasy collided with reality.

"How many animals had to die so you could wear your ugly coat, *LeWhore*?" I heard.

My chin, which was so proudly turned up, dropped immediately. I looked at the clot of evil fifth graders. Stone-cold gazes met my eyes. The fifth graders, all of them, were smirking at me with nastiness. This was the first time I'd ever heard that clever rhyming of my name with the word "whore."

"My name's *Lenore*," I said, unable to even address the issue of the teasing of my splendid coat.

"No, your name's *LeWhore*, LeWhore," one of them said.

"I have a fur coat," I tried.

"We can see that, *animal murderer. Baby seal clubber.*"

"I don't club seals!" I yelled.

"No, you club baby seals," one said.

I couldn't win. So I did what any fur-coat-wearing girl being accused of killing sweet, fuzzy animals would do. I tried to buy them off.

"Do you guys want my markers? They're pastels, not classic colors," I said.

"LeWhore is too good for the classic colors," they teased.

I returned home from school that day crestfallen and confused. I looked at myself in the mirror and brushed my fingers lightly over the rabbit fur of my coat. I stuck my hands into the muffler and spun them around the silky lining. None of it made sense. I looked amazingly sharp and superior. My coat was made of fur, Goddamnit. I took it off slowly and tucked a hanger into it, shoving the coat to the back of the closet. After the day's teasing, I could never wear it again. I placed the muffler and the earmuffs into a box and put them on the shelf in my closet. Maybe this coat and its accessories had been so grand, so completely fabulous, that they'd been just beyond the fifth graders' reach. They couldn't comprehend the coat and its cold, black rabbit fur. Its glory had surpassed their range of understanding, and all they could do was recognize that it was something they didn't know.

"How did everyone like your pretty new coat today?" my mother and father asked me at dinner that night.

"It was so beautiful and so fantastic that they couldn't even see it. I guess there must have been a blind spot of shining light where I was all day, until I took the coat off," I said.

"You're always a shining light, doll," my mother said.

"Dad, do you think I can catch cancer?" I asked him.

"You can from cigarettes," he said, puffing on his cigar while eating dinner.

I went to bed that night, dreaming of all the wonderful pity I'd receive once I caught cancer from cigarettes, just like Joanna from down the street. Maybe, after the chemotherapy was over, my hair would grow back bright red instead of mousy brown.

death and me:
a love story

I WAS IN a full panic before my mother said anything at all. I didn't want to ask what was going on, because her face and her shaking hands were confusing me. Usually, when I was in trouble, my father looked at me a certain way, and then it was clear: I'd been caught. But Dad wasn't there, and all I had to go by were my mother's ambiguous signals.

Finally, she spoke. "Your grandmother tried to kill herself today. She put a bag over her head and tried to suffocate herself."

God, I was so relieved.

Almost excited, even. I got out of school early for this. Poor Mom, though. This was her mother, and I can see getting upset over this sort of thing.

My mother had a tendency to swallow this kind of thing whole. She was literally shaking with grief. Some people get upset like this. My mother was one of these people. I guess it's safe to say I didn't inherit this particular behavior.

Because Nana tried to off herself, my brothers and I had to visit her all summer long. We'd stand outside the automatic doors of the mental institution for a while, taking in the flowery, summer air, and then enter. The whoosh of sterile, crazy-people scent replaced the outside smell, and into Nana's room we were ushered.

The halls were white. Not sterile white, but eggshell white. It was so crisp and clean. I had imagined shit on the walls and muffled screams. It was more like an elementary school without the children.

The rooms where they kept the patients didn't have open doors. I don't see why they didn't keep Nana's door open, though. It would have been hard for her to escape, seeing has how she was in her eighties and she had only one leg.

And there was Nana, crumpled on her bed. She looked like she was sinking into the mattress. There was no fat on her body, none at all. The blankets covered her torso, but you couldn't tell there was anything under there. If there hadn't been a head sticking out the top and a foot sticking out the bottom, she'd easily go undetected.

Nana didn't ever turn to see us. She knew we were in there, but she didn't care. Her face would just stay, all squeezed around her mouth, in a perpetually angry expression. She smelled terrible, like week-old urine, but so does everyone else in a mental hospital.

"Lenore, next time you come, bring your Nana drain cleaner to drink," she'd say.

"I'm not allowed to, Nana. Sorry."

Then she'd try with my brother.

"Benjamin, you're the smartest one, right? Find Dr. Kevorkian's number for Nana."

Ben was only eleven. He just quietly declined and apologized for not being more helpful.

We'd spend a long, unbearable hour in that awful, sharp room, struggling to make conversation. What do you say to a crazy old lady whom you never really knew to begin with? She blamed my mother for her attempted suicide. After all, my mother was the one who brought the fresh fruit to her in a plastic bag. She was tempting her, obviously.

We watched Nana deteriorate in the next few months. She shrank smaller and smaller, week by week. Eventually, my grandmother starved herself to death. It was different than I expected it to be. I was very unaffected by her passing. I didn't even go to her funeral.

I was surprised when my siblings told me that her death was disturbing to them. I didn't understand. I've realized since then, Death made his footprint on me long before Nana went. I was desensitized when he zapped my identical twin sister, Margot, in the womb.

The umbilical chord attached to my twin was pinched, so she couldn't get any nutrients from my mother. It also wrapped around her neck and strangled her, which was the eventual cause of death. My chord was pinched also, but not for as long as hers was. I was born dead, in that ridiculous way where I wasn't actually dead but the doctors say I was for dramatic effect. But there was no hope for my twin, who was dead three days before we were born. Dead bodies decompose very quickly, even in the womb. This means I was floating next to my decomposing sister for the last three days of my womb life. I must have smelled terrible when I came out.

The time I spent with my dead sister in the womb, I believe, forced a bizarre relationship between myself and Death. I go to sleep thinking about my mother getting into some sort of horrific accident, resulting in her decapitation, or the portioning up of my little brother on some grimy hotel room floor by the local pervert. I can't control it. I've tried to think about happy things like babies and puppies, but then those babies and puppies die. My brain forces the thoughts into visualizations, and soon I've knocked off my entire family and all my friends.

The worst part about this problem of mine is the irrational mess I become when these nighttime reveries are especially jarring. I'll start believing that these things are actually going to happen, that I'm psychic. I'll call my father and beg him not to go to any public places for a while, because there will surely be an armed madman in Home Depot or that little Argentinean restaurant. And he'll kill Mom, too, but only after he rapes her. It drives Dad crazy. "Stop calling, Lenore. We're not even going to Home Depot today."

When I think about my twin, I wonder why I ended up alive and she ended up dead. I always end up feeling some level of guilt for being alive. When I think about this topic in depth, I often feel so blameworthy that I punish myself in small degrees. I'll stay home from a party I was looking forward to or make myself watch a movie without my contacts so I get a headache. Sometimes this frame of mind moves in a circular motion. In the beginning I will think about

Margot, which results in the culpable feeling; a need to reprimand myself is created, compelling me to think about the death of a loved one.

Although Margot's death certainly did have an effect on me, it didn't offer an explanation of Death. I didn't understand it as a child, even knowing about her, and I don't understand it today. This is tremendously exasperating because I believe that, given my insider's info, I should have come up with a theory by now. In reality, I just don't know what happens—I don't even know what I think happens. I have examined all of the most popular beliefs, and none of them seem logical to me. If there is a Heaven, by now it must be packed. Under the same assumption, Hell would be overflowing with tortured souls. I could go on for hours about why these ideas have an endless string of flaws attached to them but then I feel pressured to come up with a viable hypothesis of my own. Eventually, the thought of it will drive me crazy if I don't just assume that reincarnation would be a reasonable explanation. I go with this premise only because I believe that recycling is a relatively efficient way of keeping our environment clean. The parallel may be difficult to draw but it is there if you work at it, which I do.

Today, my grandmother and my twin's deaths are still the only family deaths I have experienced, and I suppose they have both been important.

Even if it affected me in no other way, Nana's passing made me realize that I was different from others because of the loss of my twin sister. And in the end, no matter how many hours I spend upsetting myself with images of death, or how many sets of twins I see walking around to remind me of Margot, I'm not always bothered by it. I think I benefit in some way by this thing that haunts me. I sometimes think I know more, or that I'm tougher than the rest of the people my age.

I spent one summer taking courses in biology when I was in high school. In the program, we got to dissect human bodies. Real, bloated, dead bodies, and they didn't cover the faces with surgical napkins, or make any attempt to dehumanize the cadavers. While half of the class ran out of the room covering their mouths, and the ones who stayed spent the rest of the day moaning about how "all they could think about was the poor departed and their families," I was holding organs in my hand and laughing at the squishing noise that they really do make when you squeeze.

I have Margot to thank for that.

the passion of
the limbo lord

THE FIRST AND only time I ever found myself star struck, I wasn't even meeting a celebrity. Well, he was somewhat of a celebrity, but he wasn't in the movie business and he was about three thousand miles away from Hollywood.

It was in Jamaica. My parents took us to a resort there for vacation when I was in grade school. I remember being very excited to go to the Caribbean because I wanted to find out once and for all whether it was pronounced Care-a-BEE-anne or CARRIB-ee-anne. Once we arrived, however, I discovered the trip would be exciting for more than just that one reason.

We got to our rooms in the resort early in the afternoon, and we each found a slip of paper shoved under our door. It was an itinerary for the offered entertainment, shows and activities mostly.

Scheduled for the third night of our stay in Jamaica was an entertainer called, simply, "The Limbo Lord."

When I saw this, I nearly fainted. The words called out to me, jumped right off the page. For reasons I can no longer comprehend, the Limbo Lord was one attraction I felt I had to experience. I felt so strongly about witnessing this man's act that I crossed my fingers and wished to fast-forward through the first two days of vacation in order to get there more immediately. This was a sacrifice I was willing to make in order to more quickly satisfy my curiosity for the ancient art of the limbo.

I tried to keep busy for the first two days. I got my hair braided by a rotund, constantly giggling woman. She used such an enormous amount of grease in my hair when she braided it that, when we got back to Illinois, I had to wash it with dishwasher detergent seven times before it even began to come out.

I decided it was worth it because I knew I could wear it to school the first day after vacation. Everyone would know I'd been somewhere tropical and they'd be wild with jealousy.

I talked about the Limbo Lord with the giggling woman while she braided my hair. I asked her if she knew of him, and she said of course she did. Excited by her answer, I probed for any information I could get about him.

"The man can bend like he's not a human," the woman said in her thick, hardy, Jamaican accent.

This was an obvious bit of information, but still, hearing it from the mouth of someone who knew him personally made it seem like a revelation.

The night before the show, I rambled on and on about how I'd heard that the Limbo Lord was really good and that he could bend like you wouldn't believe and how amazing it all was.

My parents, who were totally unimpressed, pretended to be engaged.

"With whom are you going to go to the show?" Mom asked, with her aggressively perfect grammar.

"I'm going with Jenny and Krista," I announced, happy to prove I didn't need them. I had made friends around the resort easily because I was still young enough to think it was okay to walk right up to someone and inquire about her availability as a best friend.

"Well, I hope you girls have a nice time," Mom said.

"But remember, if the Limbo Lord is wearing loose shorts, it's best to look away," Dad reminded me.

It bothered me that my Dad would make fun of this limbo master. I had already created an image of him in my head, and he was amazing. If something did pop out of his shorts while he shimmied under that limbo bar, it seemed to me that we'd be lucky to have been among the people to witness the exposure. This was no ordinary flash of vulgarity; it was the lewd mistake of the Limbo Lord. That had to mean something.

The Limbo Lord did not wear shorts. It turned out, he was a flamboyant gay man wearing a paisley jumpsuit, seemingly designed specifically to accommodate the physical demands of the limbo.

He had a matching hat.

He started his performance with an explosion of fire on either side of his body. I imagined the fire to be symbolic of the passion he felt for the limbo. It was a very exciting kickoff.

The giggling woman was right. This man could not possibly have had bones in his body, the way he was bending. He slipped under a bar that, I swear, was no more than three inches above the ground.

By the end of the show, my jaw was on the ground and I could barely move. It was stunning to see what I had seen, a man scrunching himself into a right angle for me, just for me, just for my entertainment. It made me feel like a queen with a jester.

After a long, heavy round of applause, the Limbo Lord announced that, in addition to being a limbo master, he was also an accomplished psychic. He read palms, and he would be happy to read any of ours for only ten dollars right after the show.

A limbo master *and* a psychic? I couldn't believe my ears. It was the luckiest, most profound day of my life. I ran to the door on the side of the stage, waiting for my mind-reading Limbo Lord to emerge. I thought it inexplicable that the rest of the audience had quickly dispersed, uninterested in meeting this man.

The moment he came out was the moment I was star struck.

I couldn't speak. All I could do was stare at him with buggy eyes, like a little girl with a mental disease.

He held his hand out to me the way the Queen of England might, perhaps expecting me to kiss the back of it. I took his hand in mine and stuttered at him.

"I have t-t-ten dollars."

"Wonderful," he said, and he sashayed over to a table with two chairs, instructing me to follow with a curl of his index finger.

The Limbo Lord told me that, by reading my palm, he could see many things. He predicted love, and loss of love, things like this. Probably picking up on my disinterest in the subject of love, he switched quickly to the subject of death.

"A close friend of your mother and father will die within a year," he said.

"Which one?" I asked, very much engrossed.

"A heart condition renders him weak, but his name I cannot speak," the Limbo Lord said. Such lyrical language!

That night, I broke the news to my parents.

"Do any of your friends have heart conditions?"

"Yes, Richard does," they said.

"He's going to die this year. I'm sorry."

"Lenore, why would you say a thing like that?" my mother scolded.

"The Limbo Lord is the one who said it. I'm just letting you know as a favor so you can prepare for your loss," I said.

That year, I looked in the obituaries every day, searching for Richard's name. I questioned my mother and father about the status of his heart condition, hoping every time there would be some bad news.

I would have settled for a slight decline in health, but he stayed the same all year.

When eleven months had passed, and Richard had only one month left to get his act together and start dying, I began to worry.

I was pretty sure it took longer than a month to die from a heart condition.

In the back of my head, I knew I might have to face the possibility that the Limbo Lord was no psychic; that he was a sham. He had no paranormal powers.

The month ended.

My mother made me cupcakes because she could tell I was feeling down.

Richard had not died, nor had any other friend of my parents.

It was a major disappointment.

The Limbo Lord might have had a superhuman ability to wiggle under a bar, but he was also a con artist. I knew I had been taken.

While I licked thick, chocolate frosting off the top of a cupcake, I vowed that I would never again allow myself to be as star struck as I'd been in Jamaica. And that I wouldn't ever trust another suspiciously flexible psychic, no matter how passionate he may be about the limbo.

nana vs.
the vagrants

BEFORE MY GRANDMOTHER was too crazy to be trusted, my parents used to leave us with her when they went out of town together.

My father was a retinal surgeon, so he and my mother often used the Vitreous Society as an excuse to get as far away from their children as possible. It was absurd, but they thought we all believed them when they told us that they "just really wanted to go to that eyeball conference."

If anybody had bothered to sneak a peek at the airline tickets, we probably would have discovered that their destination city was nowhere near the Vitreous Society conference. We all played along just because we knew that we'd get away with much more when they were gone.

Nana didn't care about schoolwork like my parents did. She didn't care if we didn't drink a glass of milk with dinner. She didn't care if we even *ate* dinner. As far as she was concerned, with all of us older than three, we were ready to be shipped off to some textile factory to earn our keep.

My mother used to force us to ask Nana questions about her childhood, perhaps as some form of punishment.

"Nana, what was your life like when you were a kid?" I'd ask.

"You have to be more specific, Sara." She never knew which one of us was which. "It was like a lot of things," she'd tell me.

I'd be getting ready to go, but then I'd see my mother, sliding her finger across her throat in the "ask-more-or-you're-dead" gesture.

"What was your mother like? Did she ever threaten you?" I asked.

"My mother had me working with the sheep when I was three. There was no time for nonsense. All those sheep, and I was supposed to be a boy so I could help out with the animals. But I was a girl. All those sheep." My grandmother's childhood was similar to *The Silence of the Lambs*.

"That's fascinating, Nana." I'd look up at my mother, and she'd shake her head. *You're not finished yet.*

"What about, um, school?"

"Why are you badgering me? School was school. It was snowy and cold all year round, and school was far away. I didn't get home early enough to round up the sheep and I'd get whooped. My father wasn't there, but my brothers used chains to set me straight," she'd ramble.

"Sounds delicious," I'd say.

Having previously demonstrated her unique bond with her grandchildren, Nana was a shoo-in for the babysitting position.

When Nana was watching us, everything moved slowly. Nothing happened at a reasonable speed. We spent hours of each day waiting for Nana to shuffle from one place to another. She seemed to be weighed down with fifty pounds of necklaces and jewels. Then, when she was finally ready, she'd accuse us of not being prepared to go.

"Now, have you taken a BM? Because if we get going and then you need to take a BM, I won't be pleased," she'd warn.

"No, Nana. My B works for me. It only Ms when I want it to," I'd tell her.

I used to think BM stood for "butt movement." Same basic principle.

When she was in charge, Nana would enforce illogical rules, claiming she had her reasons and that we'd understand when we were her age. One of these rules that we'd apparently come to appreciate in a little under a century was the "bedroom rule." This law dictated that Benjamin and I were to sleep in the same bed.

In retrospect, it seems obvious that Nana only created this rule so that Ben would be my problem instead of hers if he awakened with a nightmare. Because Ben had a twin bed and I had a queen, we slept in my room.

I was a good sport about the sleeping situation until I opened my eyes in the middle of the night to Nana wiping a clot of vomit off my pillow. I sat up to find an entire puddle of puke seeping into my bed. Nana was wiping it off with a paper towel, and Ben was standing next to her, looking guilty.

"Ben had an accident. Go back to sleep," she said to me.

Go back to sleep? She wanted me to go back to sleep? The bed was hard to find beneath all that vomit. All Nana had done to ensure that the problem was fixed was scoop some of Ben's barf off the sheets. That was nice, but there was still a big wet stain on the bed, and the smell certainly didn't disappear with the scoopable chunks. Go back to sleep? I didn't think so.

Ben, on the other hand, didn't see the problem. Nana lifted the covers and he started to get back into bed—directly on top of the vomit patch—to go back to sleep.

I had to change the sheets that night. I had to get Ben a just-in-case basin, and I had to spray generous amounts of air freshener in my room to mask the evidence of Ben's throw up. Nana went back down to my parents' bedroom to dream about sheep herding.

When my parents came back from their fake conference, they brought tote bags for each of us. The bags had the Vitreous Society logo on them—a little eyeball man. Mom and Dad thought we'd believe them if they got us little eyeball tote bags, but we knew they had probably ordered them from a catalog.

I ignored my agenda of outing their real vacation, and I pulled my mother aside.

"Nana tried to get me to sleep on Ben's puke," I told her.

"What can I tell you, Lenore? Your grandmother doesn't always have her wits about her."

My mother acted cool and pretended not to be bothered by the fact that she'd just left her children with a demented old lady for an entire week, but it was clear that she knew it couldn't happen again. We wouldn't stand for it.

So the next time they went out of town, they hired an *entire family* of demented people to watch us.

There was a husband and a wife, and their two children. The kids were about our age. One was a boy and the other was a girl. Apparently my parents had taken notice of the children, and that they were still alive, and based on that information alone my parents decided that these people were qualified to move into our house while they were gone and take care of their children.

We had never met this family before they came to babysit. They weren't relatives. They weren't friends of the family. They weren't friends of friends. I'm not sure they'd even show up with the six degrees of separation. To this day, I still can't get either my mother or my father to admit to me where they found them. I have determined that the most likely place is the side of a highway in central Illinois.

"This is, um, Barb and, um…." My mother was waiting for one of them to mouth the name of the husband to her so she'd get it right.

"This is Barb and Henry," she told us. "They'll be watching you this week while we're at the Vitreous Society conference."

"We'll bring you tote bags," Dad said.

"Make it key chains this time," I challenged.

The new babysitting family was strange from the very beginning. For dinner the first night, they fed us casserole. We'd never had casserole. Our mother cooked meat and vegetables. She cooked with spices and there were usually at least four different dishes on the table to choose from. But this family made a giant, quivering mold called casserole, with potato chips crumbled on top. It was the only thing on the table.

"Where's the first course?" I asked.

"Eat your casserole," Barb instructed.

"What's for dessert?" Tim asked.

"Potato chips," Barb answered.

"But there's potato chips on top of the castle roll," Ben whispered to me.

"I know." I rubbed his back empathetically.

After we spent dinner cautiously picking at the casserole, Tim unburdened his heart to me and Ben, revealing that he had a crush on Barb. We'd never seen Ben so angry. He was positively appalled.

"I'm telling Mom," he declared.

"You can't tell Mom," Tim said. "She can't know about this. It's not like I'm going to move in with Barb and Henry. I still want to live here. I just kind of like Barb," Tim explained.

"I don't care if you love New Mom. I still love Old Mom." Ben wasn't having any of Tim's excuses.

Luckily, Tim's sordid affair ended promptly at nine o'clock that night. Barb and Henry decided we were ready for bed.

"We're going to come by each of your bedrooms to make sure that you've said your prayers," Barb said.

None of us said it aloud, but we were all thinking the same thing: *What the hell are prayers?*

We had never heard of them, but we were sure that they couldn't be good. If our parents didn't have us saying prayers, it wasn't unreasonable to think that the babysitters were trying to manipulate us into something terrible. It all seemed very devious.

Tim, Ben, and I were all in my bedroom when Barb and Henry knocked on my door that night.

"Why are you all in here?" Henry asked.

"We were just getting ready to say our prayers," I lied.

"You say them together?" Barb asked.

"Don't you?" I asked.

"Well, go ahead. Say your prayers, then," Henry demanded.

We were caught. None of us knew what to do.

Then Ben got a look about him. He always got a look about him when he was forming what he thought was a good idea.

He got up and stood on the bed. He put his fists on his hips dramatically.

"Boom boom boom boom, dubby dubby dubby dubby!" he shouted.

Quickly, Tim and I caught on.

We didn't know what the hell he was doing, but we figured whatever it was, it was just as likely to be saying prayers as anything else.

We both stood up next to Ben and repeated after him.

"BOOM BOOM BOOM BOOM, DUBBY DUBBY DUBBY DUBBY!" we yelled. We jumped around the bed, holding hands, screaming our prayer at the top of our lungs.

Barb and Henry didn't know what to think. They just quietly backed out of the room and shut the door behind them.

We got away with it that night, but for the rest of the week, we were punished. There was more casserole; there were more potato chips for dessert. We had to play with their children, who were basically like a couple of wet rags. "Catch the ball," we'd tell them before throwing it, but it just bounced off them and then they'd cry.

By the end of the week, Nana was sounding like a gift from the babysitting gods. It didn't matter anymore that she might make us sleep on vomit. We didn't mind. Just so long as she wasn't so evil as to feed us casserole and make us say our prayers.

From then on, Nana watched us when Mom and Dad went on their Machiavellian vacations. She even watched us after she got half of her leg amputated.

She'd wag the stump at us like an index finger. "If you have to take a BM, take it now," she'd nag, stump flopping up and down.

But we never complained about her again. To us, our lunatic grandmother was always better than the vagrants Mom and Dad found along a highway in Central Illinois.

spreading christmas cheer is what little jewish girls are here for

WHEN I WAS in middle school, I was part of the chorus.

See, what happened was, my mother lied to me and told me I had a beautiful singing voice.

"Oh, Lenore! You sound like an angel!" she used to tell me.

Yeah. An angel with cancer of the esophagus.

Anyway, she'd been lying to me about my singing voice ever since I was a young girl.

In grade school, in the talent show, I screeched out "Castle on a Cloud" from *Les Misérables*. I also sang a song about how mean adults are to kids, from a movie called *The Five Thousand Fingers of Dr. T.*, which was originally a Dr. Seuss book.

At this age, I identified heavily with anything boasting an abused child as its protagonist. Must have had something to do with my dirty, conniving, lying mother. In any event, all this singing and all the false praise I received for it encouraged me to join the chorus in middle school.

Part of our duties as crappy middle school singers was to go around town to old folks' homes and sing Christmas songs in December.

A school bus would take us through the cold city. I loved the way Champaign looked when it was cold outside.

At the nursing homes, the staff would wheel into the room with the television all of the melting, decrepit old people. There's always a room with a tiny, busted television in old people facilities. Some of the old people are in there for twenty hours a day. Longer, sometimes, if the staff forgets to bring them to bed. Old people have trouble moving and they can watch television for longer periods of time than any other demographic.

Our chorus would shuffle into the room, which was always cramped and suffocating, and we'd position ourselves in two rehearsed rows.

The old people would sit there, some of them excited about the deviation in their usual routine, some of them completely unaware of our presence.

Their eyes looked like they were bleeding pus. When they blinked, and they did often, it looked painful. They wiggled their dry lips. Their tongues seeped from their mouths, dragging across those cracked lips in an attempt to wet them, but there was never any saliva.

There were flies. In the middle of the fucking winter in Illinois, there were still flies. Perhaps I hallucinated them. There were flies, nonetheless.

Then we'd explode into Christmas songs, cheery and cheesy, belting them out at the top of our lungs, as the old people cried pus-filled, emotional tears.

It all made me want to vomit.

But I couldn't, because I had a solo. I had to step forward, closer to the decaying elderly, and sing a special Christmas solo while I stood there, a repulsed Jew.

I smiled so big while I sang. No one knew. No one knew I wanted to euthanize these miserable old creatures. Singing to them seemed ridiculous. As though a Christmas song was what they needed. As though a Christmas song would make them forget about the oxygen masks affixed to their faces and the colostomy bags screwed into their sides.

For Christ's sake.

The rest of the chorus wasn't so bothered. They all had grandparents. I suppose they'd grown accustomed to seeing old people melt away in a pus puddle. I did not have grandparents playing any kind of significant role in my life, and old people looked like they belonged to another species through my eyes. I did not, and I still fail to see the point in living to such an age.

When my mother's mother moved to my hometown to die, I remember watching a male nurse pull her pants and underwear down to her knees while supporting her slumped-over body on his shoulder, and then lift her to the toilet, revealing her bruised and bedsore-covered backside. I decided then that I would die before I was ever in that state.

So I hated going to the nursing homes. But at the same time, I didn't have to be in school if I went to the nursing homes, and all of my friends were in chorus with me. So I went.

Then, one day, we had a field trip to sing at another facility.

They told us it was not a nursing home, as we sat in the idling bus outside of the busted-looking building.

And they told us nothing else.

Bundled up in puffy coats and scarves, we trickled out of the school bus.

When we were all inside the building, the staff began to bring in our audience. And this is when it became clear to us that we were singing to a collection of people suffering from serious genetic diseases, deformities, and retardation. The cast-away secrets of otherwise "normal" families.

Until that moment, I didn't know places like this existed. Places for the kids who weren't perfect enough to secure a spot in the families they were born into. Sent by people who didn't want abortions, but didn't want the end product either. Those people put their deformed and retarded children into group homes like this, signing over custody to the state, washing their hands of their big, imperfect secret.

The kids in my chorus took one look at their audience and began to shake. They began to cry. They were so frightened by the oversized heads and the undersized appendages and the eyes rolling back into skulls. I don't blame them. We were in middle school, and we weren't warned. We were just shoved into a room with people whose lives were infinitely more terrifying than our own. No one else knew these places existed, either. And suddenly, we were singing to a crowd of people we thought were urban legends.

I looked at these people and felt the opposite of what I felt at the elderly homes. I felt among friends. Misfits, all of them.

Just like me and my friends.

I wasn't cast away by my family. Far from it. But I felt alone in many regards, despite their unconditional love. And these people were alone, too. And they always would be. There was no sugar-coating that.

The chorus wept while they sang. They cried because they were haunted.

I sang better than I ever did in my life.

we don't need
no education

IN THE GRAND tradition of striving to reach one's potential, my father attempted to get me into prep schools when I was in eighth grade. Dad was endeavoring to mold me into a more suitable character than I was shaping up to be by having me educated in the Northeast, which is the region of the United States in which spoiled children prepare for Yale by snorting cocaine. We spent a few weeks that summer driving from one exclusive boarding school to the next. My dad had gotten it in his head that I should go to Andover or Choate Rosemary or Deerfield or Exeter, like all of the most powerful ex-coke addicts. My dad drove with his left hand gripping the top of the steering wheel, and with his right hand he would shake a handful of sunflower seeds the way a gambler shakes dice. Every now and then, he'd toss his right hand up to his face, filling his mouth with sunflower seeds. He sorted through each and every one of the seeds, one by one, removing them from the shells with his tongue. Each time, he shifted the mouthful of seeds to the back of his mouth while situating the empty shell on the tip of his tongue. Then he'd angle his face toward the open window and spit.

I hated the sound of driving fast on the highway with the car window open. All that air rushing into the car was so loud you couldn't hear the oldies station my dad played. No matter what city we were in, my dad found the oldies station on the radio. It was as if he had some kind of supernatural gift for locating a frequency giving air time to the Shirelles. We'd drive around past fields, past the ocean, past water towers and barns and skyscrapers and strip malls, and always the oldies station played in the background.

You couldn't hear the music though, with my father's window cracked. What you could hear was the wind and, of course, the sounds of my father crunching on his seeds and spitting the shells out the window. That was all perfectly audible. I don't know how it was possible that a one-inch sliver of open window and the chewing and spitting of sunflower seeds could drown out a blasting radio, but that's how it went.

I had interviews at all of these schools, and my dad and I were using it as an excuse to have some one-on-one time. It was nice to spend the time with him, because I never did otherwise. He was working hard, and if I ever did get to see him, I only got him from dinnertime to bedtime, and then I had to share him with my mom and my siblings. I used that phrase once with my shrink—"share him with my mom"—and he took it to mean that I was arrested in the Oedipal stage of development. "You want to have sex with your father, and this makes you resent your mother tremendously," he said. He followed the statement by assessing me for any homicidal ideation I might have toward my mother. I thought it was a bit over the top.

The trip with my dad was about ten days long, and I was determined to squeeze in all the emotional bonding moments I could in that time. The only problem was that my father was not that kind of man. My dad didn't feel and emote; he lectured and led. That's where he felt comfortable. And because he didn't spend much time standing steady on emotional ground, he didn't know how to relate to me. He spoke to me as though I were his apprentice. I spent a good majority of the trip listening to Dad deliver monologues about hard work and why it's necessary. All of these speeches began with the same thing. My siblings and I had it memorized.

"If you work hard, get a good job, and make a lot of money, you can [fill in the blank]."

Sometimes my brother and I would say this to each other jokingly, but fill in the blank with something ridiculous.

"If you work hard, get a good job, and make a lot of money, you can have a rubber mold of your body made for the express purpose of filling it with freshly churned butter, which you could offer to guests when they come to your home," I'd say to Tim.

"If you work hard, get a good job, and make a lot of money, you can fund a team of Ivy League educated geologists to locate the pet rock most suitable for your lifestyle," he'd reply.

The first school we toured was Deerfield Academy. My father had taken me to Kohl's and helped me purchase an outfit to wear for my interviews. The sweater he bought me had a picture of a sun on the chest. I wore it for every single interview. The man interviewing me at Deerfield was wearing a suit and tie. I remember feeling very inadequate as he questioned me.

"Who is your hero?" he asked me.

The fact was, I didn't have a hero. There were people I looked up to, but in those same people I was aware of qualities I preferred to avoid. Who has a hero in eighth grade? I didn't know how to answer the question.

"I don't have a hero," I said.

"With all the great women out there, you can't identify even one?" he pressed.

My mind went completely blank.

"You do know the name of at least one great woman, right?" he asked, condescendingly.

I nodded.

"By all means, then. Name one for me," he said.

"Sylvester Stallone," I answered.

He paused.

"Sylvester Stallone is a great woman?" he asked.

"Sylvester Stallone is my hero," I said.

"Fine," he said. "Why is he your hero?"

I stared at him with an empty expression.

"Let's move on, shall we? Why do you think you'd be an asset to Deerfield Academy?" he asked.

"Because my parents would pay full tuition for me to attend. And I'm smart and stuff."

When I walked out of the building, Dad was sitting on a cement bench, smoking a cigar. He smiled at me.

"How'd it go?"

"Really well," I reported.

"What'd they ask?"

"Who my hero was," I said.

"Who'd you say?"

"You."

Each night of the trip, Dad and I stayed in progressively dirtier motel rooms. He was attempting to teach me a lesson about frugality, but it backfired. By the end of the trip, we were staying in the most squalid of motels, places with sticky carpets and pools full of dead squirrels. One night we stayed at a place called the Thunderbird Inn, a place that was undoubtedly the most putrid motel I've ever seen. My dad and I approached the counter to rent a room. No one was there, so I pounded on the little bell over and over again until a man with a tattoo of an octopus on his chest—which I could see clearly, as he was shirtless—came shuffling out in an aggravated fashion.

"Whatchoo want young lady?" he asked me through the wad of chewing tobacco he had stuffed in his cheek.

"I need a room," I said. My dad was by the newspaper stand, searching for his beloved *Wall Street Journal*.

"You're a little young," he said.

"I'm not alone," I said, pointing to my dad.

The octopus-man stared at my father, looked him up and down. He stared at me, chomping on his clot of tobacco.

"That your boyfriend?" he asked.

No one had ever confused my dad for my boyfriend before. I was only fourteen.

I said nothing.

He looked at my dad again. He turned up his lip and spit something black into a red plastic cup.

"We don't have any rooms with two beds," he said. "Just king."

My dad walked up to the counter.

"No rooms with double beds. Just king," I said.

"Well," Dad said.

So I slept in the same bed with my dad that night, a fact that my shrink found particularly interesting when I described the memory to him. He wanted to know how I remembered the motel room. Was it peaceful? Did it seem small? I told him that the room we rented was so rank I could barely keep the contents of my stomach internal. It was as though everything in the place was smeared with a thin coat of spoiled mayonnaise. The sheets felt damp, like we were lying on a big sponge. My shrink never told me what that meant.

By the time my last interview rolled around, I had gathered enough of a sense of rejection to just have fun with it.

"What are you passionate about?" the interviewer asked me.

"Well, for as long as I can remember, I've really been an ardent supporter of Sir Frances Galton," I said.

"Sir Frances Galton … as in the Sir Frances Galton who pioneered eugenics?"

"That's the one. I am quite a zealot in that regard. Just feverish over the whole eugenics cause," I said.

"Any particular group you'd really like to do away with?" he asked, trying to temper his reaction.

"I don't think there's any reason to keep the retards around," I said. "What good are they, anyway? Yes, frankly, I believe they're nothing but a drain on society."

"Men- ... mentally retarded people?" he stuttered.

"Oh, see, I don't really think of them as people," I said.

I walked out of the interview room and outside, where my dad was smoking his cigar. He was so reliable. I could always count on my dad to be sitting on a bench with a *Wall Street Journal* and a cigar.

"How'd it go?" he asked.

"Great," I said.

"What'd they ask you?"

"They wanted to know who my hero was," I said.

"Did you say me again?"

"No. I picked Mom this time around. You know, for the sake of keeping the scales balanced," I said.

"Yeah, you're mom's an all right lady," he said. "Good girl."

Dad was so proud of me in that moment. He allowed himself to believe that I'd succeeded. That I really shined in those interviews. And I allowed myself to bask in the parental pride my father was feeling for me, even though I knew it was only temporary. It was a great trip, seedy motel rooms aside. Dad and I drove back home with the window cracked and the sound of wind and sunflower seed consumption and the faint sound of the golden oldies. The rejection letters rolled in, one after another, and each one that arrived was another slap in the face for my father. Dad didn't want to believe that I'd blown the interviews. He had been so proud before the rejection letters arrived, and he didn't want to believe that his pride was unjustified. He decided I had been rejected because he was "only a doctor." "I should have been a senator," he said, defeated. That's how I could tell that he was profoundly disappointed.

I didn't care that I wasn't headed for an education at an exclusive prep school. I just wanted to spend time with my father. I loved his refusal to believe that I might have been the reason for the rejections, his refusal to believe that the pride he'd experienced was based on his imagination. That's how I could tell he really, really loved me.

i'm not
entirely certain

looking, living,
fucking, fighting

I LIKE TO listen to this couple in the building next to the one I live in. I like to listen to them have sex. I like to listen to them argue.

They're old. In their seventies, I would guess. They wash their dishes in the nude. I see her breasts almost every week. Sometimes, when they fight, he tells her he doesn't need her. She laughs at this.

When they don't fight, or have sex, they disappear. No noise. I don't know what they're doing, because I can only see into their kitchen window, where her breasts are on display during dishwashing time.

I know he wears briefs. He sits on his balcony in his briefs. They are usually red. He wears them with socks, pulled up past his ankles. When he comes outside, he sits on a foldable lawn chair. He doesn't have a book, or a newspaper, or a magazine, or a cigar, or a cigarette, or a drink. He's got nothing, but he sits down and stays there for up to twenty minutes.

Then he goes back inside.

Slides open the door, shuffles back in, and starts either fighting or fucking his wife.

I love them so much.

I've lived in many apartments and had many neighbors, but these are by far my favorite of all time.

My first-ever apartment was in Miami. My roommate was this drop-dead gorgeous girl who was nice to me even though I was really awkward and depressed most of the time, and when I wasn't, she could clearly hear me having sex with my college boyfriend. She and I would go out to have sushi once a week, and I once heard her defend me to a group of her girlfriends who couldn't understand how she could live with such a weird girl.

She and I had an ongoing battle with our neighbor. Our neighbor didn't like us because we once had a guest who parked in her spare parking spot for ten minutes. From that day on, it was war, war that climaxed one day when my gorgeous roommate came running to my room screaming.

"Lenore! There's a chop! A chop! There's a chop on our doorstep!"

"There's a chop?" I asked.

"A chop!" she insisted.

"What the hell is a chop?" I asked.

"A chop! A chop … of meat!" she said.

"Like, a T-bone?" I asked.

"I don't think it's beef," she said.

"A lamb chop?"

"I think it's pork!" she said.

"There's a pork chop on our doorstep?" I asked.

"And, Lenore, there's more," she said.

"There's a pork chop, and there's more?" I asked.

"I think it's rotten," she whispered.

And she was right. The neighbor had placed a rotten pork chop on our doorstep. It was accompanied by a threatening note, if I remember correctly.

From that apartment, with the meat lady living next door, I moved into an apartment with my then-boyfriend.

This was a big deal, that we were living together. My friends were all very excited and squealing like girls do, and I was silently screaming and panicking that moving in with this man meant that I would have to marry him.

A couple of my friends wanted to see the apartment before we moved in, so I took them by the place. We decided to knock on the door, just to see if I could show them the new digs. I knew the owner was supposed to be cleaning it out that day, so I assumed it would be okay.

I knocked on the door. A child answered.

I kneeled down to the ground and said to her, in a very high-pitched voice so as to capture her age-limited attention span, "Is your mommy home?"

No, her mommy wasn't home, and she shut the door on my face.

I turned around to see my friends staring at me in horror.

"Why did you do that?" they asked me.

"What?"

The little girl was apparently not a little girl, but a midget. It seemed I'd missed a couple of details that would have clued me into this fact, such as the beer in her right hand and the cigarette in her left hand.

This midget turned out to be my neighbor. And she was a very unforgiving midget. There was never a friendly moment between us. Not after I spoke to her as though she were a child.

My first apartment in Los Angeles was in a large building in Los Feliz. I moved there knowing almost no one. I was escaping Miami, the city that had thoroughly crushed my self-esteem, and I was beginning grad school for fiction writing.

My hypothyroidism was undiagnosed at this point, and as a result, I was probably thirty pounds heavier than what I weigh right now. I exercised three or four hours a day, ate apples and lettuce, and cried. For a year. I couldn't understand why I was getting fatter and fatter when every day I ate less and less and exercised more and more.

My neighbor in this building was a doctor. He was extremely attractive, and I was, in my estimation, extremely unattractive. In the elevator one day, he told me that he wanted to take me out to dinner, and he'd been working up the nerve to ask me out for months.

Immediately I became riddled with anxiety about how much more weight I would gain if I went out to dinner with him, this way-too-attractive-for-me man, because on a date I'd have to eat, really eat, and I couldn't even eat lettuce and apples. So, instead of accepting the invitation, I started crying. He didn't know what happened, so he apologized and kept his head down. I couldn't tell him the truth, so I told him my mother and father had just died in a horrible car accident.

After that, it was uncomfortable when I saw him. I wasn't yet accustomed to the emotional explosions I now frequently experience in mixed company.

These neighbors I have now—these old, naked, fighting, fucking, dish-washing neighbors—they put it all out there. And they're never embarrassed. And I know they've seen and heard things coming from my apartment that I should probably be ashamed of, but I'm not ashamed. They don't judge me. They smile at me when they go on walks.

I hope I will be like them when I'm in my seventies.

the little-person incident

I WAS IN a gas station because I needed a pack of Kool Kings. In line in front of me was a retarded dwarf. And I mean really retarded, as in mentally disabled. Now, I am lacking in every dwarf-appropriate social grace known to man. I have no idea how to behave when a dwarf, or otherwise tiny person, is nearby. I often confuse them with children and speak to them as such. Add retarded to the mix, and I'm outright socially crippled. Additionally, after all this time, I'm still not sure if this little person was a girl or a boy, or a man or a woman. I am just going to refer to her as "her" because it's easier that way. Just keep in mind that she might have been a he.

She had no hair. Just peach fuzz on top of her head. She appeared to have a cold, which was creating a mess of mucus on her face. She was attempting to purchase a Pepsi, but she was forty-eight cents short. I happened to be holding, in my hand, two quarters. She was fumbling around for a few minutes, trying to locate forty-eight cents, and I was standing behind her holding the two quarters.

I feel sorry for retarded people. It broke my heart, this scene.

I walked up next to her and placed my two quarters on the counter.

"Here you go," I said, smiling at her.

The dwarf turned her oozing face to mine. She smiled a really super-big smile at me, which allowed me to pat myself on the back for a moment for my extraordinarily altruistic character.

Then:

"Thank you. Can I have a ride home?"

I stared at her painfully for about five seconds. I made a decision.

"No," I said.

"Why not?" she asked.

This is where I started to panic. I didn't want her to think that I was grossed out by her, and that I didn't want her coming in physical contact with my car. I didn't want her to think that it made me tremendously uncomfortable to be in such close vicinity with a dwarf, never mind a retarded one. I didn't want her to think that my charitable nature was strictly limited to those actions that cost fifty cents or less. These were the real reasons I declined to take the retarded midget home.

"I don't have enough gas," I lied.

"You are at a gas station. Get gas," she quipped. Outsmarted by a retarded dwarf.

"I don't have enough money," I lied.

"I just live right over that way," she said, pointing east.

"I'm going that way," I lied, pointing west.

"Then I live right over that way," she said, pointing west.

Now, that frightened me. Before, there was a retarded dwarf who didn't want to walk home asking me for a ride. Now there was a retarded dwarf attempting to fool me into granting her access to my car, and whose motivation for this behavior was ambiguous. Petrifying.

"No," I repeated, sticking to my guns.

I bought my cigarettes with her standing uncouthly close to me. Then I walked out of the gas station, with her following unnervingly near. I tried to ignore her, but it couldn't be done. I could practically feel her.

And then I broke. I began to run. I couldn't help myself. I was more than apprehensive at that point. I was terrified. I turned around while I ran. I don't know what I expected to see. I guess I wanted to see her face, whether I had offended her or not.

The retarded dwarf was chasing me. Stubby little legs zigzagging rapidly back and forth, mucus and saliva flying off her face and into the air. She was visually livid, just absolutely irate, and determined to get me.

I got to my car, and it was like a horror movie. I fumbled with my keys. I dropped them on the ground and wasted time trying to retrieve them from under my car. My assailant was getting closer and closer.

Finally, I got my act together and opened my car door. I managed to slip in and slam the door shut right before she came, bashing into my window. Snot and spit smeared all over the window, and I screamed in terror. She was smashing her fist on the glass, hollering noise but no intelligible words.

I turned the keys with my shaking hand and started the car. She was still punching my window when I peeled out of the gas station to escape her dreadful attack.

This was one menacing retarded little person.

The incident ended there, but maybe the worst part of the whole thing was that no one believed me. I grew up in a small town, you see, and no one had ever heard of or seen a retarded dwarf living in the area. People tend to take notice of someone like that. There was Purple-Face Guy, Tanner the Wheelchair Kid, and the others, but no one knew of any local dwarfs, let alone retarded dwarfs.

Months after the episode, I was driving home from a friend's house. I saw her again, the retarded dwarf. She recognized my car, and me in it. She raised her arm and extended her pointer finger out to me. Kept it up, pointing at me, until I couldn't see her in my rear-view mirror anymore.

Chilled me to the bone.

mass hysteria
is still a big old
question mark

A LOT OF strange things have gone down, from a psychological perspective. Strange, inexplicable things.

Knowledge of psychological principles comes in handy daily, but there are some things that simply can't be adequately explained, and all the studies in the world couldn't come close to offering elucidations of bizarre happenings.

By a significant margin, obstetricians drop male babies more frequently than they drop female babies.

This is clearly noted in the statistics, yet possible rationalizations for why this might occur are weak. Is it because males are seen as stronger physically, and thus they are handled with less grace? Do male babies struggle more straight out of mommy's womb? No one really knows.

I wonder if this statistic is offensive to men.

Among the most bizarre of the behavioral oddities we've seen in our species are the manifestations of mass hysteria documented through the centuries.

Have you heard of the Dancing Plague of 1518?

This happened in Strasbourg, France. Hundreds of people were stricken with the uncontrollable, maniacal urge to dance, dance, dance. They danced and they danced, and they kept dancing for about a month, during which time a good number of these dancers died. Heart attack, exhaustion, dehydration, stroke.

These people dancing—it was unclear that they even wanted to be dancing to begin with. Many of them were frightened and displaying clear signs of terror and discomfort, and free will seemed not to apply to these people. This was not a jubilant dance; this was causing their deaths. Yet, the dancing could not be stopped.

The theory seems to be that mass psychogenic illness is caused by mass hysteria, which is caused by mass distress. The original distress would certainly be a reaction to some political, governmental, or social movement—though, unless you count protesting, I didn't see any hysterical dancing in the streets of Los Angeles when Prop 8 was inexplicably passed.

Back in 1518, though, there were problems with basic life—eating, keeping warm, illness, producing crops. I can only imagine that the threat of having little to no food during an ice storm would trigger some hysteria.

This dance hysteria has occurred a few times throughout history—it's referred to as St. John's Dance. When these outbreaks first began, the dancers were thought to be possessed by the devil. Exorcisms were held, but either they couldn't keep these motherfuckers still enough to successfully exorcise the demons, or there were never any demons in the first place, so the exorcisms were unsuccessful.

Also unhelpful were the musicians who frequently joined in with the dancers. At the time (and arguably still to this day), music was seen as a possible cure for physical maladies, so these musicians were attempting to help. But shit, I bet it was hard to be a bystander, witnessing this dance hysteria, and then the musicians joining it, and not thinking that the musicians were maybe poking fun. Just a little. And the stimulation the music provided to the mass dance hysteria likely only aggravated the situation.

A more scientific approach would blame ergotism—a type of poisoning caused by the consumption of rye infected with a fungus that contains psychoactive chemicals—the same psychoactive chemicals that appear in LSD. Ergot poisoning would result in symptoms including psychotic delusions, convulsions, and nervous spasms. It can also be fatal. This seems the most likely explanation. Only, ergotism causes convulsions and nervous spasms, not dancing. And this was dancing. This was clearly dancing. So what gives?

Recently, in 1962, another epidemic broke out similar to St. John's Dance, only this wasn't dancing. It was laughing. Maniacal, hysterical laughing. It was called the Tanganyika Laughter Epidemic, and it occurred in Tanzania. Apparently, there were thousands of people laughing—laughing unremittingly—for months. It appeared to be contagious; get too close and you'll be laughing, too. Schools were shut down, and paranoia that this mass laughing attack would spread to neighboring towns was high. These people weren't having fun. They were in pain. Too much laughing, too little rest, too little oxygen being taken in with their gasps for air between laughs. Much like the dancing, this was not euphoric; this was unpleasant.

Really, there's no explanation for any of these outbreaks. For any of this manifestation of mass hysteria.

I'm not really looking for an explanation, I suppose. I'd just like to know when the next one is coming. Because I really want to be there.

boomie brown,
sweetheart

MY DAD IS a wonderful man. I love nothing more than the feeling I get when I make him proud, or when I make him laugh. Every now and then he calls me "sweetheart," and it just melts me. Generally speaking, I'm a pretty tough chick. It's very difficult to push me toward sentimentality. But when my dad calls me sweetheart, I feel like I'm six years old, being tucked in for bed. Once, at a gas station, a homeless man approached me. He was filthy. He positively reeked of shit and vomit, and he marched right into my personal bubble. I was ready to cuss at him, tell him to back the fuck off.

"Do you have any spare change, sweetheart?" he asked me.

His breath smelled as bad as he did. He was repulsive. Rotting teeth, squalor crawling on his skin. But he called me sweetheart. I should have been disgusted. I should have felt almost molested.

Instead, I wanted to hug him. My father has turned that word "sweetheart" into a tender thing, regardless of whose mouth it's falling from. I gave the homeless man ten dollars.

When my dad was thirteen, he and his buddies were in a street gang in Brooklyn. They used to rob little old Jewish men, throw rocks through store windows, and get in fights in the streets. My father has a scar on his cheek from when someone in a rival gang smashed a bottle on his face. Imagining my father in a physical fight is very difficult for me to do, as I've never once seen him physically angry. His temper manifests in his eyes, which, I swear, turn bright red. Then he goes into his library and plays cards on the computer and mumbles things like "pathetic, abhorrent, murrmurrmurr" under his breath.

In Dad's gang, there was one kid who hadn't yet lost his virginity. It wasn't my father. My dad was a badass motherfucker—all the ladies wanted him—he, in fact, claims that he later dated Leslie Gore, who I'm fairly certain is a lesbian, and lesbians only date men if the men are badass motherfuckers, or if they're looking to toy with a man's heart because they hate men and all that they stand for. So my dad was dating her, and then he left her, broke her heart. Dumped her for my mother. And I don't blame him. My mother is ten times the woman that Leslie Gore could ever hope to be. My mom has class, unlike Leslie Gore, with her deplorable midbirthday-party tantrums.

The kid in Dad's gang who couldn't manage to get laid was, reportedly, feeling very down on himself. Perhaps he wasn't funny, or maybe he didn't know how to dress. I don't really know why he couldn't land a break. But together, Dad and his buddies decided that it was time to get this pitiful kid some ass.

They'd heard about a hooker named Boomie Brown who worked for a reasonable price. Boomie Brown liked to do her work in parking garages, in fluorescent lighting. She said it made her feel more like a doctor than a prostitute, which is an understandable preference—most people, even prostitutes, don't enjoy feeling like prostitutes. "Whatever works, baby," my dad and his buddies told her. She took my dad's virgin pal into the garage. As he stood there awkwardly, she looked him up and down.

"Mmm-hmm. I know what I'm gonna do with you, kid," she said to him.

"Uh, okay. Heh. What?"

"Honeychild, hold on just a minute, and I'll get right to it," she said.

Then Boomie Brown pulled off her panties and took a dump. Just squatted right there, and relieved her bowels under the fluorescent lighting.

"When you gotta go, you gotta go. Am I right, sugar?" she said, between grunts.

Dad's friend did not lose his virginity that night. He just wasn't in the mood. He lost it the next night, to a different hooker, a hooker named Ju-Ju.

My father told me this story in Las Vegas. We took a trip there the summer before I started high school. At one point during this trip, I was walking over scaffolding with my father, with flyers for hookers littered all around us. It was during this walk that he told me about Boomie Brown.

"Do all men have sex with prostitutes?" I asked him.

"Most of them, yes," he said.

"That's too bad," I said.

"It's just a normal male thing," he said.

"That's too bad," I repeated.

"You know, Lenore, I could sell you for a lot of money out here. You being a fourteen-year-old virgin and all. I could probably get thirteen thousand dollars for you. Maybe more," my dad said.

"That's a lot of money," I said.

"More than most people make in a year, sweetheart," he said, chewing on his cigar.

I've always remembered that, because I have a disproportionate fear of poverty, and my mind seems to enjoy taking me through the horrible ways in which my life could take a turn for the worse. Was it a mistake not to sell my virginity while I still had it, not to grab that nest egg when I could have? I don't know. All I know is that the guy I lost it to got a gift costing me thirteen thousand dollars, and I don't remember getting a thank-you from him afterward. Boomie Brown certainly didn't make that much when she straddled a john. Obviously, at this point, the benefits of prostitution do not outweigh the risk. I missed my opportunity. Gone, forever. It's okay, though. I got a doctorate instead. I assume I'll make thirteen thousand dollars at some point. And even if I don't, I have my dad, who occasionally calls me sweetheart. He might be a man who knew where to find a working girl named Boomie Brown who saw no problem with taking a shit in a parking garage under fluorescent lights, moments before she was to relieve an unlucky young punk of his virginity. But I love him. I love him because he calls me sweetheart, even when he's threatening to force me into underage prostitution for a large sum of cash.

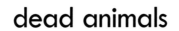

dead animals

my dead pets
are interesting

HE ASKED ME about my childhood pets, and that's where I really screwed up.

"Romeo got run over by a car," I said. "When I bent down and touched his body, it didn't move at all. I guess that makes sense, because he was dead, but for some reason I still expected his body to react to my touch. But it didn't. It just stayed absolutely stiff, like a rock covered by a layer of flesh. We all knew he was getting close to death, even before he got run over by the car, because he really stopped eating and he was suddenly very skinny. Sometimes I liked to run my fingers over his bones because it really was like he was nothing but a skeleton at the end of his life, like he'd wasted away almost completely, and when he couldn't waste anymore, he jumped in front of a car."

"I don't want to hear about how your pets died," the guy said.

I hadn't realized that he wouldn't want to hear about that. What else could he have possibly wanted to hear about my childhood pets? What's even interesting about a pet before it dies? They eat, they sleep, maybe they play with toys. The real story starts when they die.

But the guy didn't want to hear about that, and then after we talked about my pets, he didn't seem to want to hear about much else, either. I guess you're just not supposed to talk about dead animals on a first date.

I seem to have a problem. I remember only the disgusting details of events in my life, and nothing else. I don't usually find these things disgusting, but I've determined by the reactions of others whom I've spoken with that the details are disgusting, and that people would really rather I not share these details.

The issue here is this: When I weed out all the things that I would naturally include in a conversation, I am left with virtually nothing. No contributions. No pleasantries. All I have is the voice in my head screaming and screaming. *Tell her about that time you fell and broke your tooth and blood was seeping from your mouth and you were laughing and laughing and laughing! Or tell her about that guy you saw the first year you lived in Los Angeles. You know, the guy who leaned over and vomited on the head of a little Mexican woman at a bus stop!*

And then my brain adjusts itself. I remember that most people don't want to hear those stories. The girl who lives next to me doesn't want to hear about these things. She just wants to say hello like a polite person.

The girl who lives next door—I bring her up, not randomly, but because she is a problem for me. She really is. Recently, I was sitting outside with a pile of books, studying in the sunlight, getting fresh air. She came by and made the mistake of making a comment about my books.

"Studying?" she asked.

My natural response to this is to offer an illustrative description about the numerous horrible deaths I thought were more desirable than my then-current condition of "grad student."

But that's not okay. So I have to improvise.

"Yes, but I'm not very smart," I said.

I don't know why I told her I wasn't very smart. That was irrelevant. So I tried to correct myself.

"I mean, I'm not stupid, but I make a lot of really bad decisions. Especially with men. Oh, my god, I make so many bad choices! Like this one guy, my friends and I called him "The Face." There's a reason. You don't need to know why. Or maybe…. Well, the reason is because he had this face that he made…."

Around this time, my brain catches up again. I realize I'm heading toward disclosing the details people don't want to hear. So I awkwardly begin talking about washing machines, and how mine is very quiet and requires special detergent because it's a "green" washer, and if she doesn't mind, could she please tell me about her washing machine? Then she has to tell me about her washing machine, because I asked, even though I don't care, and I sit there as she answers my washing machine question with a pained look on her face, and I'm just waiting for her to get the hell away from me, just waiting for it all to end.

And this all happened because someone walked past me. It's different if a date goes horribly wrong, or if you're at a party and you get locked into a strange conversation, but this girl just walked by me and I trapped her with a bizarre interaction, with behaviors that were honestly aimed at avoiding this bizarre interaction in the first place, but ended up causing it.

This happens about once a month with the girl who lives next door. That poor girl. She probably wishes I would move already and corner my new neighbors with uncomfortable babbling.

I just wish people thought my dead pets were interesting.

beauty
in the eyes
of a fish

I HAVE ALWAYS associated certain things in my life with specific scents and aromas.

I believe it is the strongest of my five senses because I never forget a smell and I always remember the moment when I first experienced it, whereas I can just barely picture my own mother's face when pressured to do so.

Visual memories are hard to come by in the storage section of my brain. Because smells are stored in the nose, it is easier for me to hold on to them.

There is a brand of lip gloss that I cannot smell without being reminded of a trip to Six Flags in St. Louis when I was in eighth grade. I had such a good time on that trip that I often buy this brand even though it doesn't moisturize nearly as well as the other options.

Parsley, to me, smells of caterpillars. This is because my mother had parsley in her garden when I was growing up, and it was always crawling with green and yellow caterpillars. They were chubby and squishy and I hated them with every fiber of my being. The furry guys were different; they had hair, which made them more like mammals. But these slick, bald, green and yellow caterpillars did nothing but revolt me. I always plucked them off the plant and threw them into the neighbor's yard. I cannot eat parsley. If some manages to slip into my mouth accidentally, I can't help but imagine the pale white pus squirting from the body of a caterpillar as I bite down on it.

The smell of Italian sausages cooking in oil triggers memories of Donald Duck and fractions. It was a frequent scent in my house growing up, and my mouth used to water as I started my math assignment at the kitchen table. My little brother was always watching Donald Duck cartoons in the background.

The smell of wet wipes always reminds me of puppy shit.

The dusty smell of a closed-off garage forces visions of my crunched-up cat, freshly run over by my mother's car.

The smell of the house of an ex-boyfriend reminds me of the days I spent awkwardly avoiding his family because I was crying non-stop due to our breakup. There are so many, I couldn't list them all if I had an eternity.

One of my favorites, though, is the smell that brings back memories of one of my dearest friends, John. John is from the Bahamas.

He knows everything about every plant in existence. Just point at any random shrub and ask him what it is, and he'll tell you more than the best encyclopedia could offer.

He and I used to drive around Miami together and I'd point at palm trees, and he'd educate me. When I became capable of recognizing the palms for myself, I'd point to them and repeat to him what he'd taught me. John pretended to be proud of me because it was apparent that his approval was, for some reason, everything to me.

It is impossible for me to smell a rotting fish without thinking of John.

Make that any rotting sea creature, including marine plant life. This is not to say that John smells of rotting fish. But when I am around him, I smell it anyway.

In my defense, in the time I spent with him, he did handle an unreasonable number of fish. He would go wading in the ocean almost every weekend, a net in his hands so he could catch different kinds of fish. He happened to know everything about sea life in addition to plant life; otherwise I would never have trusted that these fish were safe to eat. With the things he scooped out of the ocean, John would make fish stew and soup. He didn't need to follow a recipe, but instead just knew instinctively how to prepare these things.

When we lived in the dorms, he caught small fish from the lake on campus for his fish tank.

I had a clinically depressed fish that I had purchased from a store.

It was a Betta, the kind of fish with long, flowing fins. He was blue.

When I told John I thought my fish was depressed and therefore incapable of meeting his potential, he suggested that I move him into the fish tank with all of the little campus fish.

I did, and within a week, the campus fish had beaten my fish nearly to death, chewing off his fins so he was just a drifting body.

"I don't think this particular brand of psychotherapy is helpful," I told John.

So John cut my fish's head off with a pair of left-handed scissors and flushed the pieces down the toilet. He insists that this was the most humane way of dealing with the situation, but I still think it was over the top.

John was an art major. He could re-create any nature scene and make it more stunning than real life allows. Most of his paintings were of plants and ocean creatures.

One day, he asked me to sit for a few photographs that he could use for a painting.

Sitting for paintings was nothing new to me, because my mother paints. Her art is more of a therapeutic process, however, so the paintings in which I appear are generally not flattering.

Mom also wood-burns her own frames. She has one painting of me next to a snarling wolf. The frame reads: "Lenore carefully hones her words to a keen edge before she aims and shoots them with exquisite accuracy towards those spots most tender." Or something like that.

The gist of it is, "Lenore is a bitch."

John didn't paint like that. He painted beauty, not antagonism. So I was naturally very flattered when he wanted me to sit for him.

"Don't think too much into it," he told me. "You're just the only girl I have access to right now."

But that didn't deter me from imagining myself to be a flawless princess surrounded by gentle Poinciana flowers.

I asked him daily if he had finished the painting. I was so eager to see what I looked like through John's eyes, to see if I really was beautiful enough to grace his canvas.

John and I spent a lot of time alone together, but our relationship was never sexual. It wasn't quite friendship, either, though. Within me, there was a monstrous need for his company. There was an understanding between us that I still can't fully absorb. Our friends always accused us of sleeping together, but really, we were usually bingeing on sushi and encouraging each other's bitter tendencies.

Whatever we had together, it meant more to me than most relationships I've experienced.

When he finished the painting of me, I rushed to see it. It was like looking in the best mirror in the world. Me, only far more beautiful.

"You painted me prettier than I really am," I said.

"I know," he told me.

His comments weren't meant to hurt me, and they didn't. It was true, he did exaggerate my beauty, but to me that didn't matter. He had found that beauty within a picture of me.

I was the source from which this exquisite painting originated.

It made me feel so good that I didn't smell rotting fish on John for months.

early
bedbug
trauma

WHEN I WAS young, I went through many phases. My childhood can be clearly divided into the obsessions I developed and practiced religiously. The most memorable to me were the months in which I dedicated my every waking hour to the pursuit of scientific knowledge.

In the past, I had been terrorized by insects. They were constantly popping up in places that seemed unnatural and inappropriate, like in my bed or clinging to the edge of a toilet. Come to think of it, I am currently, to this day, terrorized by insects. I suppose it was wishful thinking to delegate that to the past. I still cannot tolerate insects.

To me, there was, and is, nothing worse than curling up in your freshly cleaned bed sheets, laying your head down on the pillow and closing your eyes only to feel the tingling sensation of tiny little legs skittering across the back of your neck and into your hair.

There was one period of time in my childhood when I kept discovering strange-looking bugs in my comb after I finished fixing my hair. These were no lice. Compared to a louse, these bugs were Godzilla. I would pick it out of my comb, shudder, and hope it would be an isolated event.

But these particular bugs became all too common a sight in my hair each morning.

I looked through books to identify the bug so I could read about it. I needed to know if it was an insect that might dwell in one's hair. When I matched the species up with the bedbug, I must say, it wasn't easy information to swallow. Eventually, my anxiety about the situation grew into something of a maniacal frenzy. I scratched my head until it bled and pulled clumps of hair out of my scalp.

"They're living in my hair!" I screamed at my parents.

"Lenore, they can't be. They're too big to live in your hair. Maybe a few made their way up there accidentally, but there's no colony of bedbugs in your hair," they said.

Days went by, and I didn't spot another one.

My head appeared to be free of the bedbug infestation, but the scratching from all the psychosomatic itching left my scalp scabby and even itchier. It was weeks before the dried blood stopped falling from my head.

And after all of it, it seemed all too likely that I had imagined the whole thing.

This incident soured my relationship with bugs. They became my enemies. It didn't take them (the bugs) long to realize that they had messed with the wrong (possibly delusional) little girl. I decided to direct all of my scientific experiments in the direction of bug research. Only bugs, though. I would never hurt a real animal.

Most kids like to catch bugs and put them in jelly jars. They punch a few holes in the top and throw some sticks in there in an effort to re-create the bug's natural habitat and they try to keep the insects alive long enough to call them pets.

I did this too, but I didn't make air holes in the jar. Instead, I watched to see how long it took for them to suffocate. Then I'd document specific reaction times in a little spiral notebook.

I referred to these as my "findings."

This process was not, to me, an exciting one. It was a matter of importance in the scientific community. If I didn't run tests to see how long a certain insect could survive without air or water, who would? How would we as a people ever know? The way I saw it, my lab experiments were a necessary evil. Humans simply needed this information. Or else. Or else what? Would you really want to risk whatever the answer to this question may be? I didn't.

In another form of experimental science, I spent many summer nights in my childhood smacking lightning bugs with a baseball bat and then spreading their glowing torsos across my driveway with my sneaker. The faint light would last for up to thirty seconds when you hit the lightning bug at just the right time.

That took practice.

Once the lightning bug butts had stopped shining their brilliant light, I collected samples and placed them on slides for a microscope. My parents had bought me a science kit that included a microscope and other fun lab equipment. Hours would go by as I gathered bug guts and wings to magnify.

As a scientist, I was careful, meticulous. I cataloged every specimen, just like my father had taught me. "Real scientists catalog," he said. "Don't be sloppy with your work. If you get sloppy, you're at risk of being sued." To my father, every action should be a reaction to the possibility of getting sued. So I was careful. Just as soon as a blob of dragonfly brain was smeared across the slide, it was properly labeled and stored.

My mom let me set up my lab on the kitchen table, which is really disgusting, now that I think about it. I would carefully study each sample and sketch them in my notebook along with all of my other findings—I am a terrible artist, so most of these sketches appeared to be nothing but scribbles, but during that egomaniacal stage of development, I thought I was an artistic genius. "My God, this drawing I've done of this roach's thorax is brilliant!"

Because I had labeled them so professionally before, I was able to keep very accurate notes. The smell of the sample (sharp cheddar), the texture (bumpy), buoyancy (sometimes), and yes, even the taste of the sample (bitter apple) were all included. I should make it clear that I lied about the taste—I just made that shit up. Completely inconsistent with my claimed scientific morals, and certainly cause for a lawsuit, had this been the real deal. My dad would have been quite angry.

Whenever I came across a particularly interesting slide, I'd show my mother.

"What's this I'm looking at?" she'd ask, trying to encourage my quest for education.

"It's an ant's vagina."

"How do you know it's the genital region of the ant?"

"Because I labeled it."

"It looks red."

"Well, she was in heat. Which would explain the extreme buoyancy."

"Of course," my mother agreed.

My father, while proud that I was showing an interest in something scientific rather than artistic, was not as patient. He looked at only a few slides before becoming bored, complaining that the insides of a bug are just the insides of a bug. And sometimes that's true: The insides of a bug are just the insides of a bug. Maybe it was the truth in my father's opinion that made me lose interest in my own personal pursuit of scientific discovery. Maybe it was the fact that I felt my beginner's microscope was inadequate in its magnifying capabilities. How was I supposed to make significant scientific advances with a microscope that was stamped with a Playskool sticker?

I guess in the end I did alright, anyway.

Now when I want to kill bugs, I use Raid. I've discovered it's much more efficient. Though I don't know how I might react should my hair become infested with bedbugs again, because my understanding is that one should not spray Raid into her hair. If the Raid canister doesn't specifically mention that, however, I will certainly do it, because whatever damage it causes can be added to the lawsuit I file against them in the aftermath. Everything is going to be okay.

the
jelly fish
of christ

WHEN MY MOTHER and father took me, Tim, and Ben on vacation to Corpus Christi, Texas, they told us we were visiting the body of Christ. "That's what 'Corpus Christi' means," my mother said. Apparently, they had chosen Corpus Christi as a vacation destination not for the quality of the beaches or the breezy weather that provided escape from the snow and ice of Illinois, but because they wanted to relax in the body of Christ. This was strange, given that my family is Jewish.

Dad said we were staying in a resort, but it was more like a condo. There were two bedrooms, a living room, and a kitchen. I had never vacationed anywhere with a kitchen before. Although my home in Illinois was equipped with its very own high-quality kitchen, the fact that our condo in the Body of Christ also had one was something I found wonderful. My mother didn't like the implications of a kitchen on vacation, but for me, it was great. Somehow, in this little beachfront kitchen, everything tasted better.

It wasn't only the food. We went grocery shopping and did homework on this vacation. Everything we did in Corpus Christi, we did in Illinois. But now that we were doing it in a different, new home, it felt special. It was as though we had suddenly been put in the witness-protection program because we as a family had testified against an organized crime leader.

My mother and father took one of the bedrooms, and Tim and I took the other. Ben slept on the couch because he was the youngest. I loved that someone had to sleep in the living room. It made me feel like I was living the life of another person. I had known families that lived in houses with fewer bedrooms than there were people, and they always fascinated me. It seemed like such a noble thing, to have no private space of your own, to sleep on the couch. This condo, with its tiny kitchen and inadequate bedroom space, allowed me, for the very first time, to imagine I was worthy of pity. First, we'd been relocated by the FBI, and then we had to rely on love and family togetherness to get through the financial hardships. Of course, Ben was the most pitiful because he was the one on the couch.

It was decided that each day of this vacation, my brothers and I would have to do an hour of studying. My father was teaching me how to factor. He would write up about fifty factoring problems for me to solve, and when they were completed, I was finished. While I did my factoring, I'd watch the seagulls flying past our compact, rectangular balcony. I always did math homework on my belly, lying on the floor. The condo had soft, white carpets that I could squeeze with my toes. After an hour of propping myself up on my elbows, they were marked with the indentations of the carpet pattern.

Tim and Ben finished their homework before I did, probably because they weren't daydreaming about having to change their names and move to the Body of Christ to avoid being discovered and brutally murdered by mobsters. By the time I completed my fifty problems and Dad checked them, my brothers were practically jumping out of their skin. They wanted to get down to the beach, but they didn't want to go without me. That they refused to go without me and instead waited and waited was no surprise. When we weren't in Illinois, the three of us were very much a team. We functioned as one single unit, and couldn't have fun if we weren't all present.

The very first time my brothers and I went down to the ocean, we were shocked by what we saw. The beach was absolutely littered with the carcasses of jellyfish. There was barely enough room to lay a towel in the sand, there were so many. To some people, this was something to ruin the day, to soil the beach-going experience. To us, it was like discovering a gold mine. For hours, we examined these dead jellyfish, calling each other over when we found an especially revolting one. We were lucky; we'd seen beaches before. Dead jellyfish, on the other hand, were brand new to us.

When we got back to the condo, Dad was in the kitchen peeling a mango. He and Mom had gone grocery shopping and picked up a dozen or so because they were on sale. I had never tasted a mango before. Tim and Ben hadn't either. Watching Dad scrape the excess mango off the skin with his teeth was fascinating, because none of us had ever heard of this new, exotic fruit that could be purchased on sale in the Body of Christ.

Dad handed me the slimy, skinless mango, and it slipped around in my fingers. "Take a big bite," he said. I did, and as I chewed, the sweet flavor filled my mouth. I let mango juice drip down my cheek and onto the white carpet. I loved this new life. I loved that there were fantastic sea creatures lying dead on the shore of our beach. I loved that when we walked, we walked the surface of Christ. I loved that we ate slippery, bright orange, unheard-of fruits over the white carpet without thinking twice.

In the condo in Corpus Christi, we all loved each other. We loved each other in Illinois, too, but it was a more hostile and out-of-our-control brand of love. In the condo it didn't matter that there was no personal space because we wanted to be with each other, not hiding alone in a room away from the rest of the family.

The day after Mom and Dad brought mangos home from the store, my brothers and I went down to the jellyfish beach again. My mother had warned us not to touch them. She wasn't sure that they couldn't sting us just because they were dead. Dad said we should just touch one and find out.

"Are you going to urinate on them after they get stung?" Mom asked.

"I'll piss on Tim and Ben, but it would be bawdy of me to go on Lenore. You'll have to do her," he negotiated.

We decided just not to touch the jellyfish. Instead, we poked at them with sticks. They were soggy and falling apart. It was unexpected because they looked so stiff lying there on the sand. We didn't think the sticks would sink right into them as they did. That their consistency was different than we had imagined made us more curious. Scattered on the beach along with the jellyfish carcasses were hundreds of pieces of driftwood. Tim picked up an arm-sized log and chucked it at one of the jellyfish next to Ben. As soon as the wood hit the body, there was an explosion of jelly goop. It splattered all over Ben, covering his hair and his clothing. He was drenched in jellyfish guts.

A minute of pure silence went by, as we waited for the sting of the jellyfish to register on Ben's face. When after that minute he was still pain free, we all knew what was going to happen.

Within the next ten minutes, each of us was positively swimming in little bits of dead jellyfish. We smashed the jellyfish, aiming the spray of guts at each other. We pushed each other down into the bodies and smashed faces into tentacles. By the end of it, we were picking up entire bodies and throwing them at one another. When we were finished, we looked like the three children of the Swamp Thing, and we didn't smell too good either.

Having spent the morning engaging in a physically demanding jellyfish fight, we were ready to eat. We tried to sit down at one of the little cafés by the ocean for a hamburger and maybe a strawberry shake, but none of the restaurants would seat us. "You'll have to come back when you cease to inspire nausea," they told us.

The three of us walked back to the condo. Mom and Dad looked up from their newspapers.

"How was the beach?" Mom asked.

"It was fun," Tim said.

"What's that you're covered in?" Mom asked.

"Jellyfish," I said.

"The jellyfish can't sting," Ben reported.

"This we can tell," Dad said.

"Take a seat," Mom instructed, patting the couch cushion next to her.

And so we did. The condo in Corpus Christi had that effect on us. Maybe it was the mangos, and maybe it was the small living quarters. There was no place else on earth that the three of us could have walked into the living room, covered head to toe with dead animal parts, and still been invited to sprawl out on the living room floor without first rinsing off a bit. Similarly, there was no place else on earth that the three of us could have whipped dead animal parts at each other and been laughing at the close of the fight. There was just something about the Body of Christ that made carcass fights seem fun.

thanksgiving
pig

THANKSGIVING WITH MY family included no Thanksgiving dinner, but rather a giant pig carcass spread out on the table, looking like it'd been run over by a steamroller. It was flattened, yet crispy. When the pig cadaver had been initially placed on the table, I noted the inch and a half of pig juice it was sitting in and privately considered the possibility that the submerged portion of the beast was rather soggy.

The eyes were still in the eye sockets, because, I don't know, why waste them? I moved around the table in an attempt to avoid eye contact, but no matter where I went, the pig's eyes followed. If this were a human, we'd be having a moment. But it wasn't a human (that's good). It was a pig, and it was dead and split in half and crispy and presenting itself for my family to consume.

I don't like pig, and I don't like pigs looking at me. But, pig: It's what's for dinner.

My brothers immediately began fighting over the pig cheeks, which evidently are the most desirable section of a pig head to devour. My father followed, accusing my brothers of being sissies for not instantaneously sawing the snout off and gobbling it down. Dad ate a corner of the snout and spent the rest of the weekend eating the remainder in tiny portions, savoring it as one might foie gras. "I'm going to get some snout," he'd announce, and then he'd disappear into the kitchen, emerging minutes later chewing vigorously and smiling. After the initial dinner, we'd store the remnants of the pig's head in a Tupperware and place it in the refrigerator next to the eggs. I accidentally opened this Tupperware in an effort to locate the left-over macaroni and cheese and found the pig's decapitated head once again staring at me.

While we ate the original pig dinner, we discussed politics. We discussed judges and the fact that they rarely show preference to granting custody of a young child to a father over a mother in the case of a divorce. Being a psychologist in training, I offered my learned knowledge on this subject.

"Many analysts believe that a man can love a child, but regardless of that love, he is incapable of providing nurturance," I said.

We talked about that, and then my father finished chewing whatever segment of pig he was eating.

"I found that out with you," he said. "I found that out when I tried with all my heart to breastfeed, but no milk ever came out."

Naturally, at this point, one of my brothers took the opportunity to add:

"But it worked well when you tried with your dick!"

Ha! Jokes about receiving fellatio from your infant daughter! Good family fun! Disney material!

We weren't always this way. We used to not say things like this out loud. Perhaps the "out loud" in that statement is telling. It was always there, though it is only recently considered nontoxic to verbalize these thoughts. Because we are all grown and no longer malleable children, perhaps? Because we were tearing pieces of flesh off a pig carcass and eating them? The mere act might have soothed our defenses against such thoughts.

Thanksgiving dinner with my family is akin to eating with a group of circus clowns. Not circus clowns who juggle and make balloon animals, but circus clowns who kidnap little boys and slice them into tiny human filets, saving the ears and nose in a jar of formaldehyde.

But, still, I'd rather do that than whatever it is that normal people do. I once attended Thanksgiving dinner at a college friend's house and his mother continuously force-fed me meals I didn't want to eat, insisting that I "looked thin." I wanted to punch her in the face, but you can't just go around punching people's mothers when they feed you.

Unless it's my family. You could probably get away with it. As long as it's Thanksgiving.

a thousand words: baby birds

I'D SAY MY life started at the approximate moment that my identical twin sister died next to me in my mother's womb.

After that, it moves all over the place. But that was the key moment, right then. And it, being the key moment, has peppered every other moment in my life.

Before grade school—kindergarten, I believe—I took piano lessons with a woman whose age I cannot remember. She forbade her students to touch the keys of the piano. We were "dirty little children," and we could not be trusted to keep her piano, which was not actually her piano but the school's piano, clean. Instead, we played "Mary Had a Little Lamb," pounding out each note on the wooden plank that covered the keys when the piano was shut.

From this teacher, I learned almost no piano—not entirely surprising—but I did learn that I had murdered my twin sister. After class one day, she pulled me aside.

"No one will tell you the truth, but I will," she said. "You are a murderer. Your twin sister is dead because you made her dead when you sucked the oxygen out of her inside your mother's belly."

This, as it turns out, was not true, as one fetus cannot suck oxygen from another fetus. Because a human fetus is not a feline character in an old wives' tale. But what did I know?

I didn't know much.

I didn't know what it meant that my twin sister died before she was born. She was never born. How could she have died when she was never born? Doesn't one invariably come before the other?

On a holiday—some holiday, I can't remember which one—my mother, frazzled from being the mother of five living children and one dead child, lost focus and dropped me off for school to a locked and empty building. And she didn't come back, at least not immediately, so I took a walk. There was a path lined with Sycamore trees. There was an illness going around in Sycamore trees that season. They were all falling ill, and inexplicably dying. Their leaves withered, and their branches drooped, and, as a result, birds' nests that once comfortably rested in the crooks of the trees shifted. Sometimes, the nests would shift enough that an egg would fall from the tree.

That day, wandering alone, I came across an egg that had fallen from its nest, which had shifted from its position on the tree, which was curling up and dying. This egg had cracked in half, revealing the fetus of a bird, drooped over the edge of the shell. The shell, though open, had pieces held together by a clear film. A string of this clear film was suspended between two large pieces, and on this string rested the baby bird's crooked head.

I crouched down, hands on the ground, chin between my knees, and stared. I thought and thought and thought, and I eventually I laid belly down on the cold cement of the pathway, my face no more than a couple of inches from this tiny, dead, fetal bird.

Its skin was transparent beige. It had no feathers. Its eyes were closed. Its beak was closed. Its veins were dark. Its wings were bare. There was no blood. It just rested, broken, but not damaged, on the edge of the shell. I thought then, after watching it do nothing, after watching it be dead: "Aha! Dead without ever having been born."

And that's when I noticed just how human this little bird looked. My God, did it look human! It was nothing but a tiny little bird-human, and it had died before it had been born.

So I rolled over next to it, onto my back, and I smiled and I smiled and I looked up at the sky through the branches of the Sycamore trees that were bending and dying, releasing baby bird-humans to fall to their deaths, before they were able to be born. And it felt like they were falling all around me. Though really, none were falling, not after the first one, but Goddamnit, it felt like they were raining from the sky.

All of these birds. Dead without ever having been born. Killed by the Sycamore trees that refused to hold them carefully.

Trees can't be evil. They can't be. They produce oxygen; they give life. But these Sycamore trees were tossing these baby birds to their deaths, and they were killing them, just like I'd killed my twin sister. But trees can't be evil. And if the trees weren't evil for killing these birds, then I wasn't evil for killing my twin sister.

I used my fingernails. I clawed through the dirt in the ground beneath the Sycamore trees. I dug a hole, a nice deep hole, and I buried the baby bird inside. I put it to rest, telling the tiny bird it had not been murdered. No, it had just died before it was born, and it was okay.

That's when my mom came back to get me.

Since then, it's like these baby birds really are raining from the sky—I see them everywhere. And I dig a hole in the dirt with my fingers, and I lay these not-murdered baby birds to rest, and I tell them it's okay.

apocalyptic evacuations: d.r. haney interviews lenore zion

In August 2010, for two nights running in two locales, novelist D.R. ("Duke") Haney, another contributor to The Nervous Breakdown, had a chat with Lenore Zion on topics ranging from evolution to necrophilia to literature to the hard-to-place disfigurement of a stranger's skull. Much cheese was consumed in the first locale, and much pie was consumed in the second. No drugs, other than cheese and pie, were taken before or during this interview, though the transcript may seem to indicate otherwise.

Duke: We were talking about animals not long ago, and I was surprised to learn that you're repulsed by Koko the talking gorilla. You've got to be the only person I ever met who's repulsed by Koko.

Lenore: I really have a problem with it. I find it offensive that I should have to communicate with a helpless, creepy, sort-of human. I mean, it's cool that we've figured out a way to find out when the ape wants to play with his kitten, but I don't know why that should be my problem to deal with. Go find your kitten on your own. The moment they start speaking to us is the moment we become slaves to them.

Duke: Well, not the *very* moment. Koko has been communicating with sign language for a long time now, and I remain a slave of The Man. I can't see that rule by gorillas could be any worse than rule by The Man.

Lenore: Are you joking? You don't think it would be worse to be under the governance of a bunch of goofy-ass apes? Those ungainly gorillas will evolve, mark my words. The streets will be lined with banana peels. Everyone will be slipping and sliding all over the place. Hip fractures in old people will skyrocket. Chaos.

Duke: Will the apes themselves also fracture their hips? Will there be late-night commercials featuring ancient ape females who, reclining on bathroom floors, unconvincingly declare that they've fallen and can't get up?

Lenore: No, they're built like tanks. Anyway, even if they develop spoken language, they'll still shit outside. They're savages. Koko included. I hate apes.

Duke: So, which animals do you like? Apart from cats, I mean.

Lenore: I like all animals except for the following: apes, insects (especially fast-moving insects), slugs and snails (because of their slow movement), frogs and toads (because of their unpredictable speed of movement), those eyeless salamanders that live in caves filled with acid, clams, mussels—shellfish in general—and anything sticky or oozy that I've forgotten about. I find all of these animals decidedly atrocious. Physical contact with any of them generates a sensation, both powerful and perplexing to me, of having been molested.

Duke: I love shellfish. They're some of my favorite things to eat. I don't understand people who feel otherwise. I think they all need to die.

Lenore: Have you noticed that neither of us seems able to tolerate the existence of creatures we find distasteful? The two of us have a severe problem with narcissism. I wonder if, as children, our parents were proud to receive our evacuations. That's where it all begins, you know.

Duke: Our parents were proud when we went boom?

Lenore: Yes, exactly. And we likely believed we were offering up the most exquisite of gifts. "Behold, my boom." Or they were entirely unimpressed, and therefore we felt unacknowledged and wounded.

Duke: A variation might apply in my case. I was initially spoiled, being an oldest child. But you're—what?—the second youngest of five. I would think that your parents were bored with kids, and their evacuations, by the time you appeared.

Lenore: Absolutely true. No one ever fawned over my evacuations. It made me feel incredibly neglected. Likely the origin of my anal retentiveness in adulthood. Though I don't believe I'm arrested in the anal stage of development—I'm quite clearly orally fixated. I can't stop stuffing food into my mouth. Even when my gluttony has left me ill. I believe you witnessed my revolting consumption of a pound and a half of cheese, followed by two red velvet cupcakes this evening.

Duke: Yes, well. What cheese you didn't eat, I did. Also, I plan to eat more meat. I'm conclusively a carnivore, as are you.

Lenore: One of my favorites of your qualities. I am suspicious of those who don't eat meat with pleasure. They seem not to meet criteria for credibility. Perhaps it's the incessant preaching about the evils of meat consumption I find objectionable. Those comfortable on a pedestal are those I find laughable. Of course, I'm quite at home up there as well, so maybe this is all rooted in self-loathing.

Duke: I read somewhere that civilization owes everything to the consumption of meat. Vegetarians, like hoofed animals, are forever nibbling, and so accomplish nothing. Protein allows for long periods of work. Pyramids result.

Lenore: My people were forced to build the pyramids. Some people think the aliens were responsible. I wish the aliens were behind those things. I frequently wish the aliens would make contact with us. And by us, I mean me. I want them to come directly to me, so I feel special. But I want it done in a very public place, so I am not accused of being a lunatic, but instead worshiped as the human-alien attaché I was born to be.

Duke: Interesting. You yearn for contact with aliens, yet you fear contact with talking gorillas. I must say, you're very forward-thinking. Unless aliens really did build the pyramids, in which case you're reactionary.

Lenore: I'm worried that I'm coming off as self-indulgent right now.

Duke: Okay, well, let's talk about writing. No one is ever self-indulgent when talking about writing.

Lenore: Truer words have never been spoken. Let's see. Literature and writing. I just read Philip Roth's *The Breast*. It's quick, only about ninety pages. Phenomenally repellant and funny. He's one of my favorite writers of all time. Incidentally, he was profoundly self-indulgent in his writing.

Duke: I'm embarrassed to say that I've never read Philip Roth. I've always meant to, but I've never gotten around to it. I've also never read Katherine Dunn, except for her introduction to *Death Scenes*. Have you seen that?

Lenore: You've been telling me to read her introduction for some time. I still haven't, despite the fact that *Geek Love* has a permanent spot in my top five favorite books. I think you'd adore Philip Roth. He's very psychologically minded, and I know you appreciate that in a writer. *Geek Love* and Philip Roth's work were major influences on me as a writer. I bet Katherine Dunn loves Philip Roth.

Duke: *The Ghost Writer* is the Roth book I'd like to start with.

Lenore: I would start with *My Life as a Man*. It's a whole book about his rabid sexuality. I know you'd like that because you and I have had extensive conversations about human sexuality. This was how we first became friends. You knew what paraphilias were, and you impressed me with your use of the term "cathexis."

Duke: I was trying to impress you. I was aware, from reading your pieces at The Nervous Breakdown, that you'd studied sexology, so I reached for the one sexology term I knew, which was "paraphilia." I knew it from reading something by John Money, whom I loathe. There's a book called *As Nature Made Him* that will explain why. Basically, while being circumcised, a baby had his penis accidentally cut off, and John Money's solution was to provide the baby with a vagina, feed him with female hormones, and tell him that he was born female. It didn't work. The baby developed into a tortured young man and eventually killed himself. I've almost never heard so sad a story.

Lenore: That boy was also an identical twin—his twin brother was raised as a boy, and he eventually died of a drug overdose, I believe. I cited Money many times in my dissertation—it's unavoidable when writing about paraphilias in the academic realm. In Australia, there was very recently a person who managed to be legally declared as genderless. *Newsweek* ran a hysterical article about it, making it seem as though a plague was upon us, that gender-neutrality was some sort of rapidly spreading conundrum that would cause mass social unease when assigning pronouns.

Duke: I don't think *Newsweek* would be alone in creating, or trying to create, hysteria in the gender department. But to return to paraphilias: Do you have a favorite? The menu is, as you know, pretty extensive.

Lenore: I like the NOS (Not Otherwise Specified) category. I find it interesting when the behaviors toe the line of morality. For instance, necrophilia. Is this a victim-producing behavior? I'm not sure it is, unless you count the family of the body being defiled. The body is just a body—most states classify a corpse as "property," which means that these states wouldn't even label necrophilia a sex crime. It's destruction of property. I'm not sure necrophilia is necessarily morally questionable. It is certainly disgusting and offensive, but it could just as easily be ground beef, and isn't that just necrophilia with a cow? Which brings me to zoophilia (commonly known as bestiality). If we view animals as being far enough beneath us in the hierarchy of life that eating their flesh is acceptable, then why not employ them for sexual release? We've already established that their potential negative experience does not trump our needs. In discussing this, I seem to be arguing against my previous statements about vegetarianism without meaning to. Huh.

Duke: I've heard that necrophilia was much more widely practiced in nineteenth century than it is now. I don't know the reasons, but life expectancy might be one of them. The corpses were younger, on average, two hundred years ago than they are now, and presumably more attractive. As for bestiality, I'm sure it's much more pervasive than any of us know—or haven't you heard the urban myth about the surprise birthday party, the barking dog, and the girl who responds to the barking dog by smearing her naked body with peanut butter?

Lenore: Well, all of these paraphilias are far more common than people would like to admit. This is apparent when you take a look at the pornography industry—no one would pay to produce the "special interest" porn if an audience didn't exist to purchase it. By the way, I can't believe we're eating cheese again right now, and during this conversation.

Duke: The cheese must be eaten, and if you don't, I will. Don't cause me to become violent, Lenore.

Lenore: I would never. You are a man of significant stature. I'd get frightened. My life is like that song by The National—*Afraid of Everyone*. Everyone and everything scares me. I am panic-stricken when my own hair brushes up against my neck unexpectedly. I immediately assume there's a giant insect crawling on my sensitive princess skin. In my world, about six hours of each day is spent screaming in terror.

Duke: You would never know it. I think of you as being pretty tough, and that tough quality, whether feigned or legit, is one of the qualities I most enjoy about your writing. It's going to serve you well, I predict. Chick lit, meet your nemesis.

Lenore: Yeah, I don't see myself fitting in well with the chick lit writers. I don't think I write like a woman at all. Other than Katherine Dunn, I'm not influenced at all by any female writers. It's odd, because outside of my writing, I think I am actually quite girly. I like dresses and kittens and boys. I don't know if I'm very tough, but I get that a lot. My brother Tim always says to me, "Jesus, Lenore. You're a tough chick."

Duke: And yet, now that I think of it, I do remember you shrieking at the sight of an insect, and not even an especially frightening insect. In fact, I think it was a ladybug.

Lenore: You remember correctly. I despise ladybugs. They're beetles! Why do people like them? Just because they have spots? I don't like spots. My mother once ate a ladybug when she was a young girl. It whimsically landed in her ice-cream cone and she ate it. She said it was bitter. I, myself, always look at my food before I eat it. I feel like I should point out that we are, once more, eating. We've moved on to pie.

Duke: Yes. We're going to be obese by the end of this conversation. I already am obese, in fact.

Lenore: I frequently apologize to people in my life for my obesity. I call friends and tell them, "I'm sorry you are friends with such a giant, rubbery sloth of a human. It must be very hard for you." And then I cry and write in my journal about what my "goal weight" is, and how I might go about achieving a state of comfortable starvation.

Duke: Maybe you should go on a ladybug diet.

Lenore: I tried to fast yesterday but—whoops!—I ate a pint of ice cream and five hundred thousand French fries. Afterward, I became keenly focused on how many months pregnant I appeared to be based on the swelling in my stomach, and after that, I became convinced I was, indeed, pregnant. Being of reproductive age is emotionally exhausting.

Duke: This pie is emotionally exhausting.

Lenore: When I was a younger, my mother took me to a doctor for a checkup. The doctor told me I was "extremely fertile." I've never forgotten that. I've been suspicious ever since that my mother bribed the doctor to say that to me, so as to decrease the likelihood of teen pregnancy. How could that doctor have known? Now, in adulthood, I'm in big trouble for not having married and spawned. As though it's my fault. I don't like my pie. It's not what I expected.

Duke: That's strange. I'm enjoying my pie, even though it's emotionally exhausting. That's the kind of thing a lot of married guys say, huh?

Lenore: I want you to eat my pie for me.

Duke: I had a feeling you were going to say that. Say, did I eat the last of the cheese? I can't remember.

Lenore: We both did. We actually overstayed our welcome as we polished it off, I think. "I'm gonna hit the hay pretty soon," we kept hearing. But we kept at it, because, frankly, we don't fuck around when there's cheese to be eaten. Have I sucked you into the vortex that is my discomforting preoccupation with food?

Duke: You have recently. I'm not generally food obsessed. Most food-obsessed humans I've met have been female. Wait a minute, that's in no way funny. Did that pie somehow amputate my funny?

Lenore: I don't think it was the pie. I heard the man behind you speaking just now, and he said, very convincingly, "Kids drain their parents…. They kill them." It was a downer.

Duke: Unfortunately, he's right. Children are vampires. And you're extremely fertile, which is roughly equivalent to being a blood bank.

Lenore: That's very funny, but unfortunately I have to ignore it entirely in order to point out that behind you, there is a man with either a birth defect or the relics of some sort of traumatic head injury. He is bald, and the back of his head looks as though it is minus a skull. You can see the squiggly outline of his brain. I'm totally serious. You must turn around nonchalantly and look at this. He's wearing a blue shirt. That poor guy.

Duke: I don't think I can look. I'm already too emotionally exhausted by the pie; something like that could push me over the edge. But do you think he's possibly missing his skull because his kids tried to kill him? It would explain the previous remark made by the loudmouth, who's increasingly getting on my nerves.

Lenore: That loudmouth just said something about necrophilia! Did you hear that? It's like he knows what we've been talking about in this interview. You just saw the guy with the visible brain, didn't you? What's going on there? Is that a birth defect or an injury? I must know. I'm quite fascinated by birth defects. I discuss them at great length in my novel.

Duke: Honestly, I don't know what's going on with that guy's head. All I know is, I shouldn't have looked. I didn't realize people could grow raisins on the backs of their heads. That's knowledge I really shouldn't have.

Lenore: I wish it were socially appropriate to ask him about it.

Duke: In all seriousness, there are people who think nothing of approaching strangers and asking deeply personal and potentially traumatizing questions. I've met a few such people, and if ever there were proof of an empathy gene, they're it. They prove its existence by lacking it.

Lenore: Hey, I have an important question. Do I have any weird, eye-catching physical features? I'm really worried about that. When I look in the mirror for too long, I start to resemble a melting anteater.

Duke: You don't look anything like a melting anteater. Do I look like a human snow cone?

Lenore: If you looked like a snow cone, I would have tried to eat you already. Duke, tell a story about me and how wonderful I am.

Duke: Remember that time we went out to Malibu and we couldn't find Point Dume and you yelled at your friend Jason for giving bad directions? You weren't so wonderful that time. Except, now that I say that, it hits me that you want me to tell a story in which you come off as wonderful, not the opposite.

Lenore: I knew I was taking my frustration out on him. I said to you before I did it, "I am frustrated and I am going to take it out on Jason now." But Jason knows me really well. He's one of my closest friends. He knows to just tell me to go fuck myself.

Duke: So, do you want me to tell a story in which you come off as a wonderful? I can, you know. If I try really hard, I know I can.

Lenore: Yes, please.

Duke: [five minutes later] I really can. I know I can. I know! You asked me to eat your pie! That's wonderful, right?

Lenore: I'm hungry again. Someone feed me so I can forget about what an awful person I am.

Duke: Eat your pie.

Lenore: That pie fucking sucks. I want McDonald's.

Duke: Do they have cheese? I'd like cheese again, please.

Lenore: God, that cheese was good.

Duke: Did you see that talking gorilla a minute ago? He liked the cheese, too.

Lenore: The world is coming to an end.

acknowledgments

THANK YOU TO the following people: Mom & Dad, Sara & Tushar & Stella & Oscar, Lonny & Sara, Tim, Ben & Kate, Lisa Schroeder, Rachel Vander Weit & Chris Schulist, Mark Sandrock, Sadie Phillips & Dalibor Kostic, Cecilia Dominguez, Eric Neigher, Jason Lashever, Matt Nelson, Nina Hudspeth, Keiko Fernandez, Michael Mazochi, Simeon & Ruthie Grater, Ken & Cindy Weiss, Aaron Roseman, Jason O'Bryan, Sara Nimz Sullivan, Lester Goran, Sean Critchfield, Brad Listi, D.R. Haney, Zara Potts, Simon Smithson, Greg & Steph Olear, Julius Sandrock, Jeremy Resnick, Gina Frangello, Jim Simpson, Richard Cox, Slade Ham, Charlotte Howard, Milo Martin, Rich Ferguson, Kimberly Wetherell, Megan DiLullo, Erika Rae, J.M. Blaine, Joe Daly, David S. Wills, Ben Loory, Jonathan Evison, Justin Benton, Kip Tobin, Marni Grossman, Will Entrekin, Matt Baldwin, Aaron Dietz, Meghan Hunt, Meghan McGuire Dahn, Rachel Pollon, Reno Romero, Stefan Kiesbye, Don Mitchell, Tom Hansen, Uche Ogbuji, Tony DuShane, Joseph Matheny, the writers of TNB, the readers of TNB, and last, but not least, Wetzel & Hege.

LENORE ZION IS a proud midwest native, but she's been living in Los Angeles long enough to call sixty degrees "freezing." She is a writer and a therapist.

Check out these other titles from the  BOOKS library:

Subversia
by D.R. Haney

"Haney interweaves tiny details with weighty subjects deftly, through articles smartly ordered for just the right balance of thematic lilt and interest-holding lurch."
—Matt Cook, *Pank Magazine*

In this bare-knuckled, frankly autobiographical collection, D.R. Haney shares essays on his struggles and artistic evolution; from punk rock malcontent in 1980s New York, to B-movie actor in Roger Corman films; to screenwriter on *Friday the 13th: Part VII*; to expatriate writer in Serbia; to author of the celebrated underground novel *Banned for Life*. *Subversia* is written with the bracing candor and lyrical beauty that have earned Haney a cult following worldwide.

Paper Doll Orgy
Drawings by Ted McCagg

"Ted McCagg is a truly original thinker who really makes me laugh. And for that, I hate him."
—Conan O'Brien

For the first time, Ted McCagg's cartoons are collected where they have always longed to live: the printed page. His work, which has won him a legion of fans throughout cyberspace, is a regular feature on *The Nervous Breakdown*, and has appeared elsewhere on the web at *The Atlantic*, *The Washington Post*, and *Laughing Squid*.

BOOKS

www.thenervousbreakdown.com